TELL ME SOMETHING I DON'T KNOW

TELL ME SOMETHING

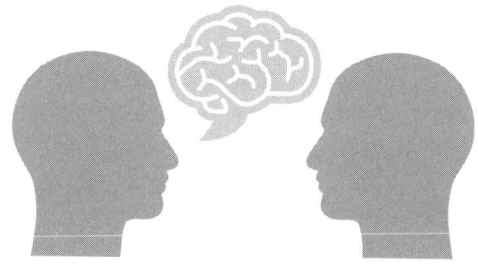

I DON'T KNOW

Dialogues in Epistemology

MICHAEL VEBER

broadview press

BROADVIEW PRESS – www.broadviewpress.com
Peterborough, Ontario, Canada

Founded in 1985, Broadview Press remains a wholly independent publishing house. Broadview's focus is on academic publishing; our titles are accessible to university and college students as well as scholars and general readers. With over 600 titles in print, Broadview has become a leading international publisher in the humanities, with world-wide distribution. Broadview is committed to environmentally responsible publishing and fair business practices.

The interior of this book is printed on 100% recycled paper.

© 2018 Michael Veber

All rights reserved. No part of this book may be reproduced, kept in an information storage and retrieval system, or transmitted in any form or by any means, electronic or mechanical, including photocopying, recording, or otherwise, except as expressly permitted by the applicable copyright laws or through written permission from the publisher.

Library and Archives Canada Cataloguing in Publication

Veber, Michael L., author
    Tell me something I don't know : dialogues in epistemology / Michael Veber.

Includes bibliographical references and index.
ISBN 978-1-55481-356-8 (softcover)

    1. Knowledge, Theory of. I. Title.

BD161.V43 2018   121   C2017-907496-2

Broadview Press handles its own distribution in North America:
PO Box 1243, Peterborough, Ontario K9J 7H5, Canada
555 Riverwalk Parkway, Tonawanda, NY 14150, USA
Tel: (705) 743-8990; Fax: (705) 743-8353
email: customerservice@broadviewpress.com

Distribution is handled by Eurospan Group in the UK, Europe, Central Asia, Middle East, Africa, India, Southeast Asia, Central America, South America, and the Caribbean. Distribution is handled by Footprint Books in Australia and New Zealand.

Canada

Broadview Press acknowledges the financial support of the Government of Canada through the Canada Book Fund for our publishing activities.

Edited by Robert M. Martin
Book design by Michel Vrana

PRINTED IN CANADA

To my parents, Nita and Ted,
for raising their boy to appreciate the philosophical value
of argumentative dialogue

Contents

Preface: *What Is This?* ix

1. Why Dialogues? *Author Meets Critic* 1
2. Fake Barns and Knowing That You Know: *Barney and Arnie Take a Ride* 7
3. Epistemic Closure: *Freddie and Betty at the Zoo* 25
4. The Paradox of the Preface: *Philosophy Takes a Stand* 43
5. Skepticism Refuted? *A Day in the Life of a BIV* 69
6. Pragmatic Encroachment: *Hanna and Rosana Case the Bank* 99
7. The Problem of Disagreement: *My Dinner with Ling* 119
8. Yet Another Gettier Problem: *Philip* 147
9. The Philosophy of Philosophical Writing Revisited: *Departmental Meeting* 163

Appendix on the Purpose and Limits of Philosophical Inquiry: *Cartesian Auto* 171

Acknowledgments 179

Index 181

Preface
What Is This?

This is a collection of dialogues in epistemology. It can be used in a course in epistemology as a supplement to a conventional textbook or collection of articles. The arguments and criticisms found in these dialogues cover some familiar ground but they also go beyond the stock objections and replies one would find in a typical textbook. Each dialogue is prefaced with headnotes that provide a succinct map of the dialectical landscape to be covered. And within each dialogue, there are margin notes and footnotes that direct the reader to the relevant literature, provide critical commentary, and a few questions for discussion. Insofar as novel lines of argument are offered and discussed here, these dialogues contain material that ought also to be of interest to the professional epistemologist. In addition, this book contains a defense of the dialogue as a form of philosophical writing—in dialogue form of course.

Why Dialogues?
Author Meets Critic

The following is the official transcript from Visiting Assistant Teaching Professor X's annual performance meeting with his department chairperson.

Author: Hello Professor. Have a good weekend?

Chairperson: Yes. Now let's get down to business. As you know, there's going to be a departmental meeting regarding your future at this institution. There's some concern among the senior faculty that you aren't working hard enough.

A: Well there is that book of dialogues in epistemology I've written. I think it would make an excellent companion book for an epistemology course. And it's pretty short.

C: That's certainly a good thing.

A: If there's a common theme throughout the work, it's the ancient project of epistemic self-assessment.

C: What's that?

A: It's the practice of determining one's own epistemic states from the first-person point of view. What do I know? How do I know it? And so forth. That's one of the oldest philosophical projects there is. In these dialogues, the protagonists assume a prominent view in contemporary epistemology and apply it to themselves.

C: What's the point?

A: To explore and test these familiar epistemological theories in a new way. And of course to examine the question of what I know and how I know it. That's why I said it's an ancient philosophical project. Remember Socrates?

C: I remember he never published anything. And the last time a meeting was held to assess his work, it didn't go so well.

A: At least they bought him a drink afterwards.

C: A real strong one.

A: Put him out cold.

C: You needn't worry about that. The senior faculty in this department haven't bought anybody a drink in 30 years.

A: Let me add that in addition to its usefulness as a textbook, this work also tries to make a few original philosophical points and arguments.

C: Good. You've got to be original in this business. It's not like you have much else going for you. But, on the other hand, there is a reason the dialogue form is as dead as old Socrates. Dialogues are a cute way to popularize a philosophical idea. But there's a reason real philosophers don't write that way nowadays. It might be good reading—sometimes—but it doesn't make for good philosophy.

A: Why not?

C: Good philosophy advances a clear position on an issue, defends it with argument, anticipates objections and then explains why the objections fail. That's what we want from students when they write papers and that's what we expect from the pros. The dialogue is just a gimmick that gets in the way.

A: But all that good philosophy stuff happens here. Positions are developed, arguments offered, objections raised, rebuttals rebuffed. I even put in footnotes!

C: To Plato?

A: It's all footnotes to Plato.

C: All of it?

A: Everything. Every idea in philosophy is just a footnote to Plato.[1]

C: I don't think things are ever that simple. Any philosophy that can be put in a nutshell belongs there.[2] That's my philosophy.

---

1 And that idea is a footnote to A.N. Whitehead, *Process and Reality* (New York: Free P, 1978), 39.
2 Hilary Putnam, *Realism with a Human Face* (Cambridge, MA: Harvard UP, 1992), 320.

A: It's nice that you can express your philosophy in just a few words. The dialogue form doesn't get in the way of good philosophy. On the contrary, the dialogue is superior to conventional forms of philosophical writing at least in some respects.

C: How so?

A: Typical philosophical writing carries a pretense that we're up to essentially the same thing as our counterparts in the natural sciences—at least under a certain naïve interpretation of what those people are up to. Problems are posed, hypotheses are offered, evidence is gathered and assessed. And the process culminates with a clear conclusion. The results are written up and the case is closed.

C: You're saying that can never be done in philosophy?

A: I wouldn't go that far. But conclusions, even negative ones, are not usually established in philosophy. And everybody knows that. To pretend otherwise is a sham. Everyone knows that too.

C: I've established all my philosophical conclusions.

A: Of course. Everyone says they've established their own conclusions. But their opponents say the same thing about the opposite conclusions.

C: That doesn't mean conclusions aren't established. It just means you have to look at the arguments. And when you look at mine, it's clear. I'm right, they're wrong.

A: I never said it's impossible to make a good argument in philosophy.

C: If you were saying that, you'd need to back it up with a good argument.

A: When I say philosophical propositions aren't usually established, I mean "established" in the way in which things get established in other fields where a result gets widespread agreement among the experts and everybody moves on. That never happens in philosophy. Sure, some ideas catch on and get taken for granted for a little while but it never lasts. You might be convinced that your arguments are rock solid. And, heck, you might even be right. But you have to know others in philosophy aren't gonna buy it in the long run. The community of philosophers will never settle on any particular set of philosophical propositions.

C: Charles Peirce once defined truth as the opinion all investigators would ultimately agree on.[3] If you're both right, then there are no philosophical truths.

---

3 C.S. Peirce, *Collected Papers 5*, ed. Charles Hartshorne and Paul Weiss (Cambridge, MA: Harvard UP, 1931–58), 407.

A: That's true.

C: And very philosophical.

A: This is why the dialogue form has always existed in philosophy. It's more honest to let the arguments run and leave things a bit open. The dialogue is philosophy stripped of its phony pretenses.

C: Well thank you for restoring authenticity to our ancient profession, Visiting Assistant Teaching Professor.

A: I'm not aiming to make improvements on philosophy. Let the profession look after itself. I have my way of doing philosophy but I wouldn't go around telling others how to do it.

C: I've noticed philosophers really like to tell each other how they ought to do philosophy.

A: Telling other people how to do philosophy is bad philosophy. They need to cut that out.

C: I see.

A: And don't get me wrong. The dialogue form isn't foolproof. Even the masters fall into pedantry with it on occasion.

C: Indeed.

A: Sometimes when you read a philosophical dialogue, you can tell the lead character is just a mouthpiece for the author who drones on and on offering his view and sprinkling in a few perfunctory arguments here and there.

C: Of course.

A: And the interlocutor adds nothing to the discussion. Nothing other than agreement.

C: That's certainly right.

A: I mean if you're going to do that, why not just write a regular old boring essay? Why pretend there's some sort of conversation going on if it's totally one sided?

C: You are correct, sir.

A: So I've avoided that sort of approach here. The best philosophical dialogues are the ones that end in *aporia* or irresolution. But that's not to say you can never tell which way the author leans. Still, the advantage of the dialogue is that it affords the author more freedom to explore contradictory positions, leave things a bit open and let the reader decide who wins. That's what a good reader will always do anyway. In the end, it's the arguments and the ideas that matter in philosophy, not the opinion of the author. I mean, why would anyone care what *I* think about this stuff?

C: You certainly make a good point there. I suppose I should give your manuscript a look before we vote on whether or not to renew your position.

A: That'd be nice.

C: Whether it's nice will depend on what I think of it.

A: When's that meeting again?

Fake Barns and Knowing That You Know
Barney and Arnie Take a Ride

Consider the following scenario:

> Henry is driving in the countryside with his son. For the boy's edification, Henry identifies various objects on the landscape as they come into view. "That's a cow," says Henry, "That's a tractor," "That's a silo," "That's a barn," etc. Henry has no doubt about the identity of these objects; in particular, he has no doubt that the last-mentioned object is a barn, which indeed it is. Each of the identified objects has features characteristic of its type. Moreover, each object is fully in view, Henry has excellent eyesight and he has enough time to look at them reasonably carefully, since there is little traffic to distract him.[1]

If we stop here, most folks would be happy to say Henry knows he is looking at a barn. But then the story takes a dark turn.

> Suppose we are told that, unknown to Henry, the district he has just entered is full of papier-mache facsimiles of barns. These facsimiles look from the road exactly like barns, but are really just facades, without back walls or interiors, quite incapable of being used as barns. They are so cleverly constructed that travelers invariably mistake them for barns. Having just entered the district, Henry has not encountered

---

1 Alvin Goldman, "Discrimination and Perceptual Knowledge," *Journal of Philosophy* 73(20): 772–73 (1976).

any facsimiles; the object he sees is a genuine barn. But if the object on that site were a facsimile, Henry would mistake it for a barn.[2]

It is widely agreed that, in these kinds of circumstances, even if he is looking at a barn, Henry does not know he is looking at a barn. He believes, with good reason, that there is a barn in front of him. And there is in fact a barn in front of him. But, the thought goes, he does not know it.[3] Since Henry is in a region where there are many fake barns, his ability to identify barns is compromised. Even though he happened to be correct, he could have easily been mistaken. Had the situation been different—had there not been fakes around—he would have known. But there are, so he doesn't.

This idea differs from traditional forms of epistemological skepticism. If you are driving through the countryside with a skeptic and you say, "That's a barn," he might ask, "How do you know it's not a fake barn?" And if you cannot answer that question, the skeptic will say you do not really know. We will face skepticism in a later chapter. For now, let us assume that common sense is correct and I can know things. What the example of Henry is supposed to show is that knowing I am looking at a barn requires not just that my eyes are working properly and that the thing in front of me is in fact a barn. To know I am looking at a barn, it must be that there are not lots of fake barns in the surrounding area.

This idea has important implications.

Farewell to Tradition. According to what is often called "the traditional account of knowledge," S knows that P if and only if (a) S believes that P, (b) P is true, and (c) S is justified in believing that P. In the 1960s, Edmund Gettier famously offered some examples that convinced most epistemologists that one could meet conditions (a), (b), and (c) and still not know. Gettier's type of example will be discussed in a later chapter. The fake barn case is seen by many as yet another counterexample to the traditional account. When Henry is looking at one of the region's few real barns, he gets a good reason to believe that there is a barn before him, he does believe it and he is right. Yet, the thought goes, he still doesn't know that there is a barn before him.

Environmental Epistemology. The environment plays a crucial role in knowledge. Someone can know there is a barn in front of him only if *there is* a barn in front of him. And that, of course, will have something to do with the environment. But the role of the environment in whether one knows that P now goes beyond P's truth. Whether you know you are looking at a barn is determined in part by whether other (apparent) barns in your surrounding vicinity are fake. To

---

2 Alvin Goldman, *loc. cit.*
3 Not everyone agrees with this. See William Lycan, "On the Gettier Problem Problem," in S. Hetherington (ed.), *Epistemology Futures* (Oxford: Oxford UP, 2006), 148–68 and "Evidence One Does Not Possess," *Australasian Journal of Philosophy* 55(2): 114–26 (1977).

generalize, you cannot know that P unless you occupy an environment where you couldn't have easily been mistaken about P.[4]

This general idea is often defended by appeal to the distinction between knowledge and lucky guesses. If I close my eyes and correctly guess that there is a barn up the road, this is not knowledge. I happen to be right but I got lucky. The idea here is that Henry got lucky too—even though he was not just guessing. Since his environment is one where fake barns abound, he could have easily ended up looking at one of them and he would have thought that it was a barn too. So, the thought goes, he got lucky and thus he does not know.[5]

The KK-Thesis. The KK-thesis says that if S knows that P, then S knows that S knows that P. If you know something, you also know that you know it. If it is true that Henry does not know he is looking at a barn because there are fakes around him, then we have an argument against the KK-thesis. A subject in a normal environment might know that he is looking at a barn. But he cannot know that he knows this unless he also knows that there are not fakes in his general vicinity. And, at least some of the time, if not most of the time, people will not know that. So knowing does not guarantee knowing that you know. Moreover, knowing does not even *put you in a position* to know that you know. A typical subject in typical circumstances can know he is looking at a barn without even being in a position to know there are not fake barns in the surrounding area.

Second-Order Skepticism? It is one thing to say that knowing does not, by itself, put one in a position to know that one knows. A second-order skeptic goes even farther. This is someone who thinks we can *never* know that we know. The driving thought behind the fake barn case may not take us that far. But it does seem to make second-order knowledge rather difficult.

Whither Epistemic Self-Assessment? Whither Philosophy? Socrates tried to get people to stop and reflect upon what they really know. Descartes's project in the *Meditations* is similar. Both exemplify a classic philosophical approach to epistemology. The idea that Henry does not know he is looking at a barn might threaten the legitimacy of this sort of traditional philosophical project. Reflection alone will not tell you whether you occupy an environment conducive to knowledge.

The Value of Knowledge. Knowledge is supposed to be a good thing. But why? For instance, why is knowing that P better than just truthfully believing it as the result of a lucky guess? This is a problem that goes back to Plato's *Meno*. Henry truthfully believes he's looking at a barn but he does not know it. But, given that

---

4 This is often called the "safety" condition on knowledge. For an overview see Dani Rabinowitz's entry "The Safety Condition on Knowledge" in *The Internet Encyclopedia of Philosophy* http://www.iep.utm.edu/safety-c/#SH4b.

5 For more on knowledge and luck, see Duncan Pritchard's *Epistemic Luck* (Oxford: Oxford UP, 2005).

Henry's belief that he is looking at a barn is true, why should he care that it isn't genuine knowledge? We might try to transform Henry's mere true belief into knowledge by tearing down the fake barns in his environment. Supposing our efforts succeed, in what way would it make Henry any better off?

This is sometimes called "the swamping problem." The worry is that, on certain conceptions of knowledge, the value of a true belief will "swamp" any value knowledge might have.[6] But it is also widely agreed that knowledge is more valuable than mere true belief. So what gives?

In this chapter, we explore the countryside with an environmental epistemologist. Along the way, we will also explore the limits of the position and challenge some commonly held ideas about what it entails. You will notice that one of the interlocutors, Barney, is fond of reasoning like this: That's a barn. Therefore, that's not a realistic fake barn. Some philosophers believe this sort of inference is illegitimate. We will address this idea in a later chapter.

Barney and Arnie are on a Sunday drive in the country. The area is populated with what appear to be (and in fact are) barns.

Arnie: Don't mess with the AC. You're going to get barbeque sauce from those boneless wings all over the dials.

Barney: Boneless wings. What a joke. It's not a wing. It's a deep-fried chunk of breast meat. They should be sued for false advertising. Used to be, nobody wanted the wings. You couldn't give 'em away! Everybody wanted the breasts. Now we're selling breasts and calling them "boneless wings."

A: You're saying it's a fake wing?

B: Exactly. And everybody's selling them. We're surrounded by fake wings. I can't believe people are stupid enough to fall for it. Not me though. I still know a real wing when I see one. I don't care how many fakes you're selling. Oh, check out that barn.

A: You say you can spot a fake wing. Is that a fake barn?

B: That's a barn. Therefore, it's not a fake barn.

A: I imagine some fake barns look real. Does that make you doubt that it's a barn?

B: No. Why should it? If that's a barn then it's not a fake barn. If it's not a fake barn, then it's not a realistic fake barn either.

---

6 Jonathan Kvanvig discusses this problem at length in *The Value of Knowledge and the Pursuit of Understanding* (Cambridge: Cambridge UP, 2003).

A: It's not a realistic fake barn only assuming that you are right in the first place about it being a barn. So you know it's not a fake only if you know it's a barn. But do you really know it's a barn?

B: I dunno.

A: What?

B: Look. That's a barn. And I believe it's a barn. In order to know something, it's not enough that you get it right. It's got to turn out—among other things maybe—that you've formed the belief in the right sort of environment. That's what I don't know. I don't know whether I've met the environmental condition on knowing.

A: What's that?

B: In order to know something, your environment has to be such that you couldn't have easily been wrong. In this case, for me to know that's a barn, it's gotta be that there aren't a bunch of fake barns in this area. Because if there are, then we're in an environment where my ordinarily reliable barn identification skills can't be trusted. And that's what I don't know.

Environmental Epistemology

A: Why not?

B: My reason for thinking that's a barn is my perceptual experience of it. And that certainly doesn't show anything about whether any *other* barns around here are fake.[7] How could it? So maybe I know it's a barn, maybe I don't. But, either way, it's a barn. That's so whether or not *I know* it's a barn.

A: I'm getting lost.

B: Where's the map?

A: Not that kinda lost. What's the issue of whether there are fakes in the surrounding area got to do with whether that's a barn?

B: Nothing. That's a barn. Therefore, if there are fakes in the vicinity, that's a barn. Like I said, that's just a straightforward sound argument. Whether there are fakes in the vicinity is only a factor in whether *I know* that's a barn. You see, if there are fake barns around here, then we're in an environment where

P. Therefore, if Q then P. This is a valid inference in classical logic. But it is unintuitive enough to be designated a "paradox of material implication."

---

7 On some views, looking at a barn can enable you to know there are not fakes in the vicinity. For a criticism of this idea see my "Knowing What's Not Up the Road by Seeing What's Right in Front of You: Epistemological Disjunctivism's Fake Barn Problem," *Episteme* 12(3): 401–12 (2015).

my barn identification abilities aren't reliable.[8] And that will prevent me from knowing. I started talking about possible fakes in the vicinity only after you changed the subject from whether that's a barn to whether I *know* that's a barn.

A: Do you *think* you know that's a barn?

B: Although I meet all other conditions for knowing that's a barn, I don't know whether I've met the environmental condition. That's a barn but, for all I know right now, there are a bunch of fake barns around here. Now since I don't *believe* that I know that's a barn, I don't *know* that I know that's a barn.

A: What would it take for you to say you *know* that's a barn?

B: I'd want a reason to think we're not in fake barn county.

A: Fake barn county?

B: Yeah. You know those fake building façades they use in old Western movies? Imagine a county where they make movies and so there's lots of those around. The barn I just saw was a real barn and therefore not a fake. But that doesn't mean the surrounding area is not full of fakes. So, before I'm willing to say I *know* that's a barn, I'll need a reason to think this isn't a fake barn county.

A: How do we get that?

B: Keep driving down the road here and I'll keep identifying barns. I'll say "that's a barn" each time I see one. If they are in fact barns, then I'll know of each one that it's a barn and therefore not a fake. This will put me in a position to know that there aren't fake barns in this general vicinity. After we do that, I'll be willing to say I know that's a barn.

A: Wait a minute. If we are in a county populated with fake barns, you're going to head down the road and you're going to say "that's a barn" and you're going to be wrong. At the end of the road, you'll think you aren't in fake barn county and you'll be wrong again. So isn't your method for determining you aren't in fake barn county no good?

Is there a way to make Arnie's point without demanding an infallible method?

B: Provided we aren't in fake barn county, the method gives me a way to know that we're not in fake barn county. Of course, there could be some poor sap

---

8 According to some, your being justified in believing that P is a matter of having formed your belief that P via a reliable process, a process that produces true beliefs most of the time. The *locus classicus* for this sort of position is Alvin Goldman's "What Is Justified Belief?", in *Justification and Knowledge*, ed. George Pappas (Dordrecht: Reidel, 1979), 1–23. One might regard the environmental condition as an additional requirement on knowledge over and above belief, truth and justification or, if one is a reliabilist, one could build it in to the justification condition and understand the notion of a "reliable process" in a way that includes reference to the environment.

who is in fake barn county and, for similar sounding reasons, thinks he isn't. And he'll be wrong. But that's just to say that the method is fallible. All methods are fallible, Arnie. We're only human. So let's head on down the road here and look for some barns.

A: But how, at the end of the road, will you know you aren't the poor sap who just *thinks* he knows he's not in fake barn county?

B: Provided I'm not in fake barn county, I'll know I'm not by this method. So I'll also know that I'm not some sap who IS in fake barn county and thinks he isn't.

A: You keep saying "provided we aren't in fake barn county" we'll know this and that. But how do you know that we've met this condition?

B: Of course I don't know I've met that condition now. How would I know whether or not we're in fake barn county until we take a look around?

A: Lemme try this. Earlier you said that even if there are fakes in the vicinity, that's a barn.

B: That's right. That's a barn. Therefore, if there are fakes in the vicinity, that's a barn. A sound argument if ever there was one.

A: Suppose we do see some fakes down the road. Will that lead you to doubt that one there is a barn?

B: I guess so.

A: And that's something that could happen. I mean, it could turn out that we spot fake barns all around this place.

B: Yeah. That's why we're taking a look.

A: If it goes that way, if we find lots of fake barns, you will then doubt that thing right there is a barn.

B: Absolutely. And it will be rational for me to do so—even though it is true that that's a barn. Sometimes it's rational to doubt things that are true. Let's hope that doesn't happen here.

A: But why would it? You just said that if there are fakes in the vicinity, then that's a barn.

B: Yeah. That's right. That's a barn. Therefore, if there are fakes in the vicinity, then that's a barn. Sound argument.

A: Okay but ordinarily when you have a conditional statement—if P then Q—and you learn that its antecedent is true—you learn P—you conclude that its consequent is true—Q. Right? And here you've got a conditional statement: if there are fakes in the vicinity, then that's a barn. Why would learning the antecedent of this conditional make you doubt the consequent? Isn't that the opposite of how conditionals are supposed to work?

> *P: Therefore if Not-P then Q.* This is another paradox of material implication.

B: Your name's Arnie. Therefore, if your name's not Arnie, I'm a monkey's uncle.[9] That's another sound argument. Should I get good evidence that your name's not Arnie—for example, if you tell me that your name is really Renaldo and you've only been pretending your name is Arnie to hide from the cops—I shouldn't infer that my nephew is a monkey. Instead, I should give up my belief that your name's Arnie and, with it, my belief that if that's not your name then I'm a monkey's uncle. That's so even if your name really is Arnie and you were just pulling my leg about being on the lam. The same happens here. If there are fake barns around here, that's not one of them. That's a barn. But if I learn that there are some fakes around here, I should give up my belief that that's a barn and, with it, my belief that if there are fakes in the vicinity, then that's a barn.

A: Why not just think that that's a barn *and* there are fakes in the vicinity? According to you, if we see fakes in the vicinity, that's what's true.

B: Here's the problem. There not being lots of fakes in the vicinity is a necessary condition for my knowing that's a barn. Remember the environmental requirement on knowing? If I say "that's a barn but there are many fakes in the vicinity" you are going to force me to say "that's a barn but I don't know it" and that, my friend, is Moore-paradoxical.

A: More what?

B: Not more. Moore. As in G.E. He pointed out that there are things that sound absurd that aren't really contradictions. Take the conjunction *It's raining but I don't believe it* or the conjunction *dogs bark but I don't know it*. Neither of those is a logical contradiction. In fact, there are plenty of things that have the form *P but I don't believe that P* or the form *P but I don't know that P* which are true. But how can something that's true sound so absurd when you say it? That's the mystery.[10]

A: Okay. Now what's this got do with barns again?

---

9 Roy Sorensen, "Dogmatism, Junk Knowledge and Conditionals," *The Philosophical Quarterly* 38(153): 433–54 (1988).
10 For further discussion of this issue, see *Moore's Paradox: New Essays on Belief, Rationality, and the First Person*, ed. Mitchell S. Green and John N. Williams (Oxford: Oxford UP, 2007).

B: Earlier I said if there are fakes in the vicinity then that's a barn. You asked what would happen if I learned the antecedent of this conditional. I said I'd give up my belief that that's a barn and I'd toss out the conditional along with it. Now you see why. There not being fakes around here is a precondition of my knowing that's a barn. So if I accept *that's a barn* and I accept *there are fakes around here*, then I'll have to accept that *that's a barn and I don't know it*. You won't trick me into saying anything like that. If there are a bunch of fake barns down the road, it will be true that *that's a barn but I don't know it* but I can't rationally believe something like that.

A: Why?

B: A conjunction of the form *P but I don't know that P* can be true but, if it is, there's no way I can know it. If I know the conjunction *P but I don't know that P* then I know that P and I know that I don't know that P. It's pretty easy to get a contradiction out of that.[11] Now since I can't ever know anything of the form *P but I don't know that P*, I shouldn't believe anything of that form either. And I should avoid saying stuff like that too. Likewise for *P but I don't believe that P*. This goes a long way toward solving Moore's mystery.

A: But didn't you kick this whole conversation off by saying "that's a barn but I don't know it"?

B: No. What I said was, "That's a barn but *I don't know that I know* it." Totally different.[12] You see, Moore's paradox doesn't extend to cases where you assert that P and then deny second-order—whoa! Look at that: a cherry '69 Camaro. Sweet.

A: Do you know it's not one of those new retro Camaros? They look a lot like the old ones.

B: Do lots of people drive those around here?

---

11 Proof:
   1. $K(P \text{ and } -KP)$ assumption
   2. $KP \text{ and } K-KP$ K-distrubution (Closure)
   3. $K-KP$ and-elim
   4. $-KP$ factivity of K
   5. KP and-elim

12 David Sosa advances the opposite idea in "Dubious Assertions," *Philosophical Studies* 146(2): 269–72 (2009). He says statements of the form "P but I don't know that I know it" are just as paradoxical as the original first-order instances of Moore's paradox. Barney disagrees.

The pair head down the road covering the entire county. Barney looks out the window at what appear to be (and are) barns. Each time he says and believes "That's a barn." After doing this for a while he arrives at the (true) belief that he is not in fake barn county.

B: Okay. We aren't in fake barn county. So earlier when I said that's a barn. I knew it was. And you see that red building right there. I know that's a barn too. You were worried about my little qualification "provided we aren't in fake barn county,...." Well you can put those worries to rest, Arnie. It's true. We aren't in fake barn county.

A: Do you *know* that we aren't in fake barn county?

B: That's a barn. That over there's a barn and that one too. So it's true that we aren't in fake barn county. Now in order for me to *know* I'm not in fake barn county, I'd have to meet another environmental requirement. I would have to be in an environment where I couldn't have easily been wrong in my belief that I am not in fake barn county. Now, this isn't fake barn county. But what if there are other counties around here that *do* contain a lot of fake barns? Maybe this is a fake barn state but we just happen to be in one of this state's few real barn counties. That would mean that although *it is true* that this isn't fake barn county, I don't *know* that this isn't fake barn county because we could have easily ended up in fake barn county. Just from driving around this one county, I can't tell whether neighboring counties have lots of fake barns or not. So I'm not yet ready to say I *know* I'm not in fake barn county.

A: Can we fix that?

B: Sure. Let's keep driving and check out some other counties. When I see a barn, I'll say, "That's a barn." After we've checked enough of the other counties in the vicinity, we'll not only know that this is not a fake barn county, we'll know that none of the counties around here are either. That will mean we couldn't have easily been wrong in thinking that we aren't in fake barn county.

The two drive around other counties. Barney sees lots of what appear to be (and in fact are) barns and each time says/believes "that's a barn." They cover the whole state and some of the counties in neighboring states.

B: Okay, my earlier belief that I was not in fake barn county couldn't have easily been wrong. This is not a fake barn state. So when I first formed the belief that I was not in fake barn county, that was something I knew because I couldn't have easily ended up in a fake barn county. I know the county we're in right now isn't a fake barn county either. That feels pretty good. Oh, look! A barn.

A: Do you know that's a barn?

B: Yep.

A: Do you know *that you know* that's barn?

B: I believe I know that's a barn. It's true I know that's a barn. And, given that we are in a real barn county in a real barn state, I couldn't have easily been mistaken in thinking I know that's a barn. So sure. I know it and I know that I know it.

A: So what you're saying is, even though there is this environmental requirement on knowledge, it's still possible for you to know that you know things.

B: That's right. It might take a bit of thought and some gas money but I can do it.

A: Something still bothers me. I keep thinking about that poor sap driving around fake barn county. Imagine he's in a fake barn state too. He looks at a bunch of fake barns and says "that's a barn." His buddy is asking him the same set of questions I asked you. He answers the same way giving exactly the same reasons. So this guy thinks he's looking at a barn and, after driving around a little while, thinks he knows he's looking at a barn and, after driving around a while more, he thinks he knows *that he knows* he's looking at a barn. But he doesn't know jack! Doesn't that bother you?

B: The guy you're taking about is totally screwed. But that's his problem—not mine. What's that guy got to do with me? I know I'm not in fake barn county so I know I'm not that chump.

A: But couldn't that guy say the same thing?

B: Sure, he could *say* he knows he's looking at a barn and he could *say* he knows he's not in fake barn county. But he's mistaken. Now, when I say that stuff, it's true.

A: But doesn't thinking about that guy make you a little reluctant to go around saying "I know that's a barn"?

B: Why would it? I'd be out of line in saying that's a barn if I didn't know that it was a barn. But I do know that's a barn. Now I'll admit, I first said "That's a barn" back before we'd established that I knew I was looking a barn. At that time, I did not know that "that's a barn" was an appropriate assertion because—at that time—I did not know whether there were fake barns in the vicinity.[13] And if there were, then I wouldn't have known "that's a barn" was true when I said it. But, as we now know, there weren't any fake barns in the vicinity when I first said "that's a barn."

Second-Order Knowledge
Barney's argument here moves quick. Given his view of knowledge, what are the conditions for knowing that one knows? Does he meet all of them? Does he know that he meets all of them?

The Knowledge Account of Assertion: It is appropriate for you to assert that P only if you know that P.

This idea is controversial. What happens to the rest of Barney's position if the knowledge account of assertion is false?

---

[13] For more on the knowledge account of assertion, see Matthew Weiner, "Norms of Assertion," *Philosophy Compass* 2(2): 187–95 (2007).

A: But you didn't know it was a barn at the time?

B: You're not listening. When I first said "That's a barn" I *knew* it was a barn. But I didn't know that I knew it. I took a certain risk in saying that's a barn on that first occasion. But we take that risk every day, Arnie. We often know what we are saying is true but it is rare that *we know that we know* that what we are saying is true. This is because we rarely know that we have met the environmental requirement on knowing. It's not impossible but it's rare. You see, life is all about risk, Arnie. You dance with the Devil and—oh hey look, a barn.

A: Where is "Rock City" anyway?

B: I think it's in Michigan.

After several more hours of driving, our heroes enter a tiny county far over the border into another state when: the unthinkable.

B: Holy crap. A fake barn! I saw the front and I was all "that's a barn," but then you swerved to avoid that armadillo and I caught a different angle and—the sucker's got no sides! So that right there, that's no barn my friend. It's a friggin' façade!

A: Okay, this is what I was talking about earlier. If I hadn't swerved off the road you wouldn't have noticed it's a phony. So you would have believed it was a barn. And youdda been wrong. Right?

B: Right.

A: So what do you say about those things you were calling barns back when all of this started?

B: What do you mean what do I say? Those were all barns.

A: Hold on. Imagine I swerved to avoid an armadillo way back then and imagine that you had the same sort of experience you just had. I mean, couldn't that have happened with that very first barn you saw? Isn't that a possibility?

B: Depends on what sense of "possible" we're using here, Arnie. Of course there is a metaphysical possibility here. There is a possible world where those were all fake barn façades and I just never caught the right angle on them. But since I know that those were barns, I know that this is a *mere* possibility. The actual world isn't that one. The situation you're imagining is a metaphysical possibility but not an epistemic possibility. It is ruled out by what we know because we know those were barns.

How far are Barney and Arnie from the first barn they saw? Does it matter to what he says here?

A: But how? We didn't see them from every angle.

B: Since when does knowing that x is an F require seeing x from every angle, Arnie? If you go that way, you're gonna end up a total skeptic. And you aren't a total skeptic are you? Now, you ask, how do I know that those earlier buildings were barns? Do you really want to go through all that again? Those were barns and I knew it and after a bit more driving I knew that I knew it. But that one there, that's a fake. What's the problem?

A: Let's try this: Do you know that's a fake barn?

B: Hmm. Well it is fake. And I believe it's a fake. But now in order for me *know* that it's fake, it would have to be that there aren't a lot fake fake barns in the vicinity.

A: Fake fake barns?

B: Yeah you know, real barns that are made to look like mere barn façades with the use of mirrors and holograms and stuff.

A: Why would someone do that?

B: Maybe it's an effective way to ward off would-be barn burglars? In any case, that right there, that's a real fake not a fake fake. But, for all I know, this county's littered with fake fake barns. So keep driving. If I see another fake barn, I'll be like "that's a fake barn." Provided that we aren't in fake fake barn county, I'll be able to say I know that's a fake barn.

A: Still seems like we're making a mistake here, Barney.

B: I'm sure you'll lemme know what that is when you figure it out. Meantime, let's ride. You got any Merle for that tape deck?

A: You think this is my first road trip? Wipe your fingers though.

Several hours and many miles pass while darkness and fatigue set in on our heroes.

A: We should find a place to stop and sleep. But there's nothing around.

B: There's a barn. Why don't we just crash in there?

A: Do you know that's a barn?

B: Don't even start. That's a barn and we need a place to bed down. I'm not going to bother driving all over another county to determine whether *I know* that's a barn. That's a barn. Therefore, it's a barn even if we find fakes in the vicinity. Who cares whether or not I know it?

A: That's it!

B: That's what?

A: That's what's wrong with your epistemology. *It undermines the value of knowledge.* At first I thought that the problem here was that your epistemology doesn't allow for second-order knowledge. But we can know that we know all sorts of stuff on this view. You wanna know that's a barn? Take a look out the window! You wanna know that you know? Drive around some more and keep lookin'! And, you're right, your view allows that we can know that we know. In fact, it's all pretty easy.[14] It's not that we can't know that we know. *It's that no one should care.* I mean look at our situation here. We need a place to sleep. That's a barn. Do we *know* that's a barn? *Who gives a crap?* Even if there's a bunch a fake barns around here, that's still a barn. Why should we lose any sleep over whether *we know* it's a barn? And why should *anybody ever care* whether he knows anything? As long as you're right, you'll get to Larissa either way. Why bother with all the extra driving around? You've got no answer!

B: Okay. But how is that my fault? Things that fall short of knowledge can have all the same practical advantages as knowledge. Like you said, you'll still get to Larissa whether you know it or just truthfully believe it. You are no better off with knowledge than you are with mere true belief. That's a fact.

A: I'm not sure about that. Think of it this way. One guy *knows* the way to get to Larissa is the path on the left, another guy *merely believes* the left is the way to go.[15]

B: Why doesn't the second guy know it?

A: Doesn't matter. Let's say he believes it as a result of a lucky guess. But the first guy, he really knows. Now imagine also the path kinda loops around and meanders. The guy who just *believes* he's on the correct path will more be more likely to start doubting that he's going the right way whereas the guy who *knows* he's on the right path will truck on. The guy who knows has a better chance of getting there because the guy who merely believes is more likely to think he's lost and turn around.[16] So at least sometimes knowledge has

---

14 This is similar to a point made by Richard Fumerton in "Skepticism and Naturalistic Epistemology," *Midwest Studies in Philosophy* 19(1): 321–40 (1994).
15 This example comes from Plato's *Meno*.
16 Timothy Williamson, in *Knowledge and Its Limits* (Oxford: Oxford UP, 2002), 62, uses a different example to make the same point.

practical advantages over mere true belief. And maybe the point generalizes. True belief leaves you to wander; knowledge ties you down.[17]

B: I guess that's better if you're into that sort of thing.

A: What sort of thing?

B: Being tied up.

A: Down.

B: Exactly. Now, in your little story, how does the one guy know he's on the right path?

A: The left path.

B: Yeah but how does he know that's the right one?

A: I don't know—*third base!*

B: Nice.

A: Let's say he knows because he looked at a map. But, like I said, the other guy just makes a lucky guess.

B: But then the guy who knows knows more than just the bit about which path gets him to where he wants to go. He knows there's a map that says this is the way to go. And since he looked at the map, he knows that the path twists and turns and doubles back a few times because that's what the map told him.

A: So?

B: So your example cheats. What's keeping knowledge boy from turning around is not the mere fact that he knows he's on the correct path. It's all the other information he has. Your example doesn't really show knowledge is more stable than true belief because, the way you've got it rigged, it's not a fair fight. If you really want to prove that knowledge has more value, you've gotta let the other guy have that same information in the form of mere true belief. So let's imagine our ignorant true believer doesn't just truthfully believe he's on the correct path. Let's suppose he also truthfully believes—by way of a series of lucky guesses—that the path loops around and that there's a map somewhere that says this is the way to go and so on. I don't see why the true believer would be any more likely to feel lost and turn around. Both will expect the path to turn and double back. When it does, they'll both keep walking. Or you could think about it from the other side. Suppose somehow that the *only thing*

> If we are careful to match the one subject's knowledge that P with a mere true belief that P in the other subject, will it always turn out that the true believer's belief that P is as resistant to misleading counterevidence as the knower's?

---

17 This is close to how Socrates answers this problem in Plato's *Meno*. There the claim is that knowledge is "tethered" in a way that true belief is not.

knowledge boy knows is that this is the path to take. He doesn't know anything about what the maps say or what shape the path is or any of that other stuff. Once the path starts looping around in crazy directions, there's no reason knowledge boy would be any less likely to doubt he's going the right way. Just because you know that P, that doesn't mean you won't lose your knowledge if things start to get weird.

A: Well this business about getting to Larissa is kind of a red herring anyway. I'm not just talking about the *practical* value of knowledge over things that fall short of it here, Barney. I'm talking about the *epistemic* value of knowledge.

B: The what?

A: Epistemic value. You see there are really two different kinds of questions about the "value" of knowledge. First, there's the question of the practical or instrumental value of knowledge—the question of why we should think knowledge is better than various things that fall short of it *at getting us other stuff we want*. But then there's this other problem—the problem of what theoretical, cognitive, or *epistemic* value knowledge has over those lesser things. In other words, knowledge has a distinct *kind* of value[18]—other than merely practical—and your view can't account for that.

B: And why is that again?

A: Say you've got two cups of coffee from different coffee makers.[19] Both cups are equally tasty and delicious. The only difference is that one of them came from a crummy coffee maker that usually turns out bad coffee. So one of the cups is good but that's a fluke—it could have easily turned out awful. The other cup couldn't have easily turned out bad because it came from an impeccably reliable coffee machine. Given that both are equally tasty and delicious cups of coffee, why prefer the one over the other?

B: If all you're looking for is a good cup of coffee on this one occasion, no reason. So what?

A: Suppose on the one hand, you've got a true belief that the path on the left takes you to Larissa. But this true belief was formed by looking at a road atlas that is full of bad information. And this is one of the very few cases where the atlas happens to be right. Now over here let's say you've got the same belief

---

18 For more on this point, see Duncan Pritchard, "Recent Work on Epistemic Value," *American Philosophical Quarterly* 44(2): 85–110 (2007).
19 This example comes from Linda Zagzebski, "The Search for the Source of Epistemic Good," *Metaphilosophy* 34(1–2): 12–28 (2003).

except it was produced in a reliable way. This belief was formed after looking at an impeccably reliable road atlas.

B: Okay, so both are true but one belief isn't knowledge and the other is.

A: Now why, given your epistemology, should we think the latter belief—the one that is an item of knowledge—is *better* than the former?

The Swamping Problem

B: And by "better" here you don't mean better at getting you to Larissa?

A: No, that's practical value. I mean *epistemically* better.

B: I've got a pretty good handle on what it means to say that something has more practical value than something else. I also understand what it means to say that something is *morally* better than something else. That's not what you're talking about here.

A: No, I'm talking about epistemic value.

B: I don't know what that is. But it sounds made up.

A: Philosophers have been talking about it for years, Barney.[20]

B: That's supposed to make it sound less made up? Lemme put it this way. I get that "epistemic" is an adjective that means something like "of or relating to knowledge." But I don't get what knowledge-y value would be—if it's not some kind of practical or maybe moral benefit that knowledge is supposed to have.

A: That's exactly my point. Somebody like you can't see what makes knowledge better—epistemically better that is—than just plain old true belief. For you, whatever properties there are that are supposed to distinguish knowledge from mere true belief, their sole purpose is to enhance truth-conduciveness or reliability. But if we've already got truth, reliability adds no epistemic value.

B: But that's only a problem if "epistemic value" is something I should care about in the first place. Of course, one of these beliefs you're talking about is knowledge and the other isn't. So in that sense one is better at being knowledge because it *is* knowledge. But that's trivial.

A: You can't see why anyone would value a belief that's knowledge over one that isn't when the sort of value in question isn't practical or moral?

B: Some people like knowing things. If knowledge is some sort of goal for you for whatever reason then yeah, you'll think it's better to know than not. But

---

20 See Adrian Haddock, Alan Millar, and Duncan Pritchard, *Epistemic Value* (Oxford: Oxford UP, 2009).

that's still a practical benefit. If knowledge isn't one of your goals, it may not matter unless knowledge is better at getting you something else you want. I still don't see how we get any interesting or objective notion of "epistemic value" out of any of this. So I don't see how this is a problem for my own view of knowledge or anybody else's. Think of it this way. You've seen *Total Recall* right?

A: *Get to zhe choppah!*

B: Does he say that in there?

A: He says that in all of them.

B: So you can actually go on holiday in Larissa or you can just have a false memory of it planted in your brain. Which of these has more "vacationistic value"? Well one of them really is a vacation in Larissa and the other isn't. So if that's all you mean, then obviously the first one. Now maybe all you really want is to *feel* like you've been to Larissa and you don't care whether you really went there or not. In that case, you might prefer the latter because you get it a lot quicker. There's no problem about accounting for the difference in "vacationistic value" between these two cases. Now to carry over the point over, one of these things is knowledge and the other is just—you want me to help with that barn door latch? Maybe if you jiggle it like this and then—

A: Whoa.

B: I can't see a thing in here but it sure don't *smell* like no barn façade.

A: I call hay loft.

B: You can have it. I gotta get outta here. I'll go back and sleep in the car.

A: I saw a boneless wing on the floorboard a while back if you're hungry.

B: You know it.

A: Night, Barney.

B: Night, Arnie.

Epistemic Closure
Freddie and Betty at the Zoo

In a logically valid inference, the truth of the premises absolutely guarantees the truth of the conclusion. Suppose you know proposition P is true. And you know P entails Q. From these, you draw the conclusion that Q is true. This seems like a foolproof way of coming to know that Q is true.

This general idea has come to be called "deductive closure" for knowledge. It can be stated this way:

> Closure: For any subject S and any propositions P and Q: If S knows that P is true and knows that P entails Q, then, evidentially speaking, this is enough for S to know that Q is true.[1]

In other words, if you know something and you know that thing entails something else then you are in a position to know the other thing too. Just make the inference.

Two prominent epistemologists who deny Closure are Fred Dretske and Robert Nozick. We will focus on Dretske. Dretske's reason for rejecting Closure stems from a deeper idea about what is required for knowledge. According to him, you can know something only if you have a "conclusive reason" to believe

---

1 There is a good bit of debate over how to state various epistemic closure principles. For an overview see John Collins, "Epistemic Closure Principles" in *The Internet Encyclopedia of Philosophy* http://www.iep.utm.edu/epis-clo/. This particular statement of closure is taken from Fred Dretske's "The Case against Closure," in *Contemporary Debates in Epistemology*, Matthias Steup, John Turri, and Ernest Sosa (eds.) (New York: Blackwell, 2005), 13–25.

it. Dretske has his own way of understanding what makes something a conclusive reason. He defines that as follows:

> R is a conclusive reason for P =df R would not be true unless P were true (in other words, if P were false R would be false).

Dretske allows both beliefs and perceptual experiences to serve as reasons. (If you find it a bit odd to call a perceptual experience "true" or "false," you can understand the definition above to say that R "obtains" or "does not obtain" when we are talking about perceptual experiences.)

An example will help make this notion of a conclusive reason clear. Suppose you believe that the used car you just bought is in perfect condition because that's what the salesman told you. On Dretske's view, the fact that the salesman told you the car is in perfect condition is a conclusive reason for believing the car is in perfect condition only if:

> The salesman would not have said the car is in perfect condition unless it were true that the car is in perfect condition.

In other words:

> If the car were not in perfect condition, then the salesman would not have said so.

If you want to know whether the used car salesman has provided you with a conclusive reason, ask yourself whether he would have said it if it weren't true. (Well, would he?)

Now consider another example: You are at the zoo looking at what appears to be, and in fact is, a zebra. Based on your visual experience—that of a four-legged equine-shaped black and white striped mammal—you believe that there is a zebra in front of you. This visual experience will be a conclusive reason only if the following condition holds:

> If there were not a zebra in front of you, then you would not have had that perceptual experience.

How do we tell whether a counterfactual conditional statement like this is true?

A common way to think about counterfactuals is in terms of possible worlds or alternative ways things might have been. There was a zebra in front of you but there might not have been. How would things have looked to you if there were not? Assuming everything is normal at the zoo on this day—your eyes are working properly and you are not prone to hallucinations or anything like that—then, it seems, if there were not a zebra in front of you, you wouldn't have had that sort of experience. If there were nothing at all in front of you or if there were some other zoo animal there, then you wouldn't have had the visual experience you did. So it looks like we can say that your perceptual experience qualifies as a conclusive reason to believe that's a zebra.

This in essence is Dretske's account of perceptual knowledge. Your perceptual experiences can give you a way to know things about the world around you because they can provide you with conclusive reasons. Now here's where things get interesting. Consider a cleverly painted mule—a mule expertly airbrushed to look just like a zebra. Is your current perceptual experience, an experience as of a four-legged equine-shaped black and white striped mammal, a conclusive reason to believe that the thing before you is not a cleverly painted mule? If the answer is yes, then the following is true:

> If there were a cleverly painted mule in front of you, then you would not have had that perceptual experience.

But this, Dretske tells us, is false. If there were a cleverly painted mule in front of you, one that is painted up to look just like a zebra, your perceptual experience would have been the same. You would still have had a visual experience of a four-legged equine-shaped black and white striped mammal. And therefore your perceptual experience does not provide you with a conclusive reason to believe that the thing in front of you is not a cleverly painted mule.

Now consider the following argument:

1. That's a zebra.
2. If that's a zebra then that's not a cleverly painted mule.
---
3. Therefore, that's not a cleverly painted mule.

This is a deductively valid argument. The second premise is true by definition. Painted or not, anything that is a zebra is not also a mule. You know that. And you also know that the first premise is true. "That's a zebra," we are assuming, is in fact true and, for reasons given above, you have a conclusive reason to believe it. So you know each of the premises and you know that the inference is valid but, Dretske contends, you cannot know the conclusion because you do not have a conclusive reason to believe it. You do not have a conclusive reason to believe that thing in front of you is not a cleverly painted mule. If there were a cleverly painted mule there, your visual experience would be the same. This is why Dretske rejects Closure. You know the above premises, you know they entail the conclusion but you don't know the conclusion.[2]

Some contend that this position is absurd. Keith DeRose puts the point by saying that Dretske's view generates "abominable conjunctions."[3] For example: "I know that's a zebra but I don't know it is not a cleverly painted mule." This seemingly absurd statement is a consequence of Dretske's view.

Although its consequences strike some as absurd, Closure denial does have its advantages. Imagine you are at the zoo admiring what you believe to be (and in fact is) a zebra. A skeptical philosopher attempts to spoil your fun by asking how you know it isn't a cleverly painted mule. You might think you can't know something like that (after all, a cleverly painted mule would look pretty much the same to you). That might lead you to think you don't really know it is a zebra, and that might ruin your whole afternoon. But, on Dretske's view, you can know it is a zebra even if you cannot know it is not a cleverly painted mule. Closure denial provides grounds for an interesting response to skepticism. (You should be able to see how Dretske-style closure denial can help with the classic problem of the brain in a vat. We will revisit brains in vats in a later chapter.)

In this chapter, Freddie and Betty are at the zoo admiring what they are both convinced is a zebra. Freddie is a Closure denier and Betty is rather critical of that position. The worry about various kinds of abominable conjunctions as well as a few other worries are explored.

Freddie and Betty are at the zoo standing in front of the zebra exhibit.

Freddie: 4:30 already? I guess we missed feeding time.

Betty: I didn't realize you were hungry. Want some of this popcorn?

F: Is there anything on it?

B: "I can't believe it's not butter."

F: You can't *merely* believe it's not butter.

B: One taste and you *know* it's not butter.

---

[2] Astute readers will notice that the above argument has two premises and the Closure principle offered earlier was stated in terms of a single premise. If this is bothersome, note also that the second premise is true by definition and can be dropped out without affecting the overall point. One might also regard proposition P in the Closure principle as the conjunction of 1 and 2 above. Closure principles for very long deductive arguments will be considered in the next chapter.

[3] Keith DeRose, "Solving the Skeptical Problem," *Philosophical Review* 104(1): 1–52 (1995).

F: "Fortified with 14 essential vitamins and lubricants."

B: Well at least the animals here are good. Take this exhibit right here. Now *that* is a zebra.

F: Indeed my friend. Indeed.

B: But we came here to see the mule exhibit. We better move on. I don't know where the mules are, Freddie, but I know they're not here. I know that's zebra.

F: That's right Betty. You know it's a zebra but of course, you don't know it's not a cleverly painted mule.

Abominable Conjunction

B: A what?

F: A cleverly painted mule.

B: A mule with a paint job.

F: That's right. And I'm not talking about some $99.95 Earl Scheib-can't-believe-it's-not-a-zebra job here, Betty. I'm talking about a mule that's been expertly airbrushed to look *exactly* like a zebra. If there were a cleverly painted mule here, you'd never know just by looking at it.

B: Why would anybody paint up a mule and say it's a zebra?

F: A zoo might do something like that in the event of a zebra shortage. Who's gonna pay 18 bucks for a zoo ticket if there's no zebras?

B: That seems pretty far out.

F: Yeah it is far out. Completely implausible even. But just because it's far out and completely implausible doesn't mean we know it's not happening. Have you checked with the zoo authorities? Did you examine the animal closely enough to detect such a fraud?[4]

B: I guess not. But wait. Are you saying I *don't know* that's a zebra?

F: Don't be ridiculous. Of course you know that's a zebra. But you don't know it's not a cleverly painted mule. I don't either.

B: Well if I don't know it's not a cleverly painted mule how do I know it's a zebra?

F: Well, duh. You're standing here looking at it.

B: What?

---

[4] Fred Dretske, "Epistemic Operators," *Journal of Philosophy* 67(24): 1007–23, 1016 (1970).

F: Here's the thing, Betty. Since that's a zebra and you know what zebras look like and there's nothing wrong with your eyesight, you know, by standing here looking at it, that that's a zebra. But since cleverly painted mules look just like zebras, you can't know, by standing here looking at it, that it's not a cleverly painted mule. Same goes for me.

B: Wait. If that is a zebra, then it's not a cleverly painted mule. Right?

F: Correct.

B: And it is a zebra.

F: Yep.

B: And *I know* that it's a zebra? And *I know* that if it's a zebra then it's not a cleverly painted mule?

F: That is my position.

B: I can see how somebody could know that's a zebra, know that if that's a zebra then it's not a cleverly painted mule but fail to know that's not a cleverly painted mule because he never puts the two together and makes the inference.

F: Yeah that's one way it could happen. But even if you make the inference, you still cannot know that's not a cleverly painted mule. At least not by looking at it and reasoning from there.

B: Let's test this out. I'll take my knowledge that that's a zebra and combine it with my knowledge that *if* that's a zebra, then that's not a cleverly painted mule. And then, via modus ponens, I'm gonna arrive at the belief that that's not a cleverly painted mule.

F: Go for it.

Betty closes her eyes and strains for a moment.

B: There. Did it. Now I know that's not a cleverly painted mule.

F: No you don't. You believe it. And you arrived at that belief by a valid inference from premises you know are true. But you are in no position to know you arrived at a true conclusion.

B: Hold on. Take look at the argument I just ran through. Here it is again. Premise One: *That's a zebra.* Premise Two: *If that's a zebra then that's not a cleverly painted mule.* Therefore: *That's not a cleverly painted mule.* That is a valid argument. Right?

F: Yes.

B: So unlike some philosophers, you're not some sort of "deviant logician" who goes around denying the validity of modus ponens.[5]

F: Not at all. My logical tastes run nice and conventional.[6]

B: And my premises are true too, right? I mean that is a zebra and if it's a zebra then it's not a cleverly painted mule.

F: Of course.

B: So we've got here a valid argument with true premises.

F: Yeah that's right.

B: Is the conclusion true?

F: I don't know.

B: You don't know.

F: Yeah that's right. I don't know.

B: But you agree that the premises are true and, since the premises are true and it's valid, there's no possible way that the conclusion can be false!

F: I know what validity is, Betty. The argument is valid. So the only way the conclusion could be false is if a premise is false. But the premises are both true.

B: So is the conclusion true?

F: I don't know.

B: I'm starting to feel like I'm standing in front of the tortoise exhibit.[7] Let's try this: That's a zebra. If that's a zebra then that's not a cleverly painted mule. Therefore, that's not a cleverly painted mule. Now, is that a *sound* argument?

F: The argument's valid. And the premises are true. Is it sound? I don't know.

---

5 See Vann McGee, "A Counterexample to Modus Ponens," *Journal of Philosophy* 82(9): 462–71 (1985) and William Lycan, "MPP, RIP," *Philosophical Perspectives* 7: 107–22 (1993).
6 See Dretske, "The Case against Closure," 13.
7 In Lewis Carroll's essay "What the Tortoise Said to Achilles," *Mind* 4(14): 278–80 (1895) the tortoise is presented with an obviously valid argument with true premises. He believes the premises but refuses to believe the conclusion. Achilles insists that if you believe the premises, then you must believe the conclusion. The tortoise responds: that sounds like another premise—better put it in the argument! Achilles obliges. Achilles tells the tortoise if he accepts the premises then he now must certainly accept the conclusion. The tortoise says this too sounds like another premise; better put it in the argument. And so it goes.

B: But you do know that all it takes for an argument to be sound is that its premises are true and it's valid?

F: Of course I know what makes an argument sound. Any valid argument with true premises is sound. And this is a valid argument with true premises. But I don't know whether it's sound. Why is that so hard to understand?

B: Maybe because you are contradicting yourself?

F: Nope. I'd be contradicting myself if I'd said that's a zebra and that's not a zebra or the argument is sound and it isn't or something like that. What I said is I *know* that's a zebra and I *know* that if that's a zebra then it's not a cleverly painted mule. But I'm in no position to know it's not a cleverly painted mule. That's not only consistent but true. I'd be guilty of logical inconsistency only if I also held some general principle to the effect that, for any subject S and any propositions P and Q, if S knows that P and S knows that (P entails Q) then S is in a position to know that Q. But this sort of closure principle is precisely what I reject.

B: Well it sure sounds like you are contradicting yourself.

F: There are things that it sounds absurd to say that aren't really contradictions. It's often true that it's raining but I don't believe it. But it's always absurd for me to say such a thing.

B: Moore's paradox.

F: You got it. Now I'm happy to admit that there is a sense in which it is absurd to *say* that you know that's a zebra but you don't know that's not a cleverly painted mule. My view entails that things like that are true. But so what? Just because something is conversationally inappropriate that doesn't mean it's false.[8]

B: Well if no one should ever say "I know that's a zebra but I don't know that's not a cleverly painted mule" why do you keep doing it?

F: Sometimes I care more about saying something true than saying something appropriate. Philosophers face that choice every day, Betty.

B: I care about truth too. That's why I'm willing to infer the conclusion "that's not a cleverly painted mule" from the premises "that's a zebra" and "if that's a zebra, then that's not a cleverly painted mule." The premises are true, the argument's valid, so the conclusion's gotta be true too! That's my philosophy.

---

8   Dretske, "The Case against Closure," 17.

F: That's chutzpah, not philosophy.[9]

B: A guy who says—with a straight face, mind you—that a valid argument with true premises might be unsound is gonna say *I've* got chutzpah? Oy vey!

F: Lemme think about that again. *That's a zebra and if it's a zebra, it's not a cleverly painted mule. Therefore it's not a cleverly painted mule.* Yes, I said that this argument is valid and has true premises but I don't know whether it's sound. That sounds pretty silly to me now.

B: So now you think the argument is sound?

F: Yes.

B: And sound arguments have true conclusions?

F: Of course. It's a sound argument and all sound arguments have true conclusions.

B: So is the conclusion true?

F: I don't know.[10]

B: Maybe we should start looking for that mule exhibit, Freddie.

Betty and Freddie walk around and look for the mule exhibit.

B: Wait a minute, Freddie. Why are we walking around? After all, maybe that was a mule back there in the exhibit marked "Zebra."

F: That's not a mule. That's a zebra. You and I both know that. Of course, we don't know that's not a cleverly painted mule. But we know it's not a mule.

B: Hold on, Freddie. Even if you are right and I know it's a zebra but don't know it's not a cleverly painted mule, how could I know it's *not a mule* but not know it's not a *cleverly painted* mule? Cleverly painted mules are still mules. If it's not a mule, it's not a cleverly painted mule.

F: Knowledge requires conclusive reasons. R is a conclusive reason for P if and only if R would not be the case unless P were the case. Wasn't that implied in what I said before?

B: I guess. But how does it explain how I can know that's not a mule but fail to know that's not a cleverly painted mule?

---

9 Dretske, "The Case against Closure," 24.
10 Freddie is here offering what I call a "logical abomination." For more, see Michael Veber, "The Argument from Abomination," *Erkenntnis* 78(5): 1185–96 (2013).

F: Your reason for thinking that's a zebra is that you had a certain type of visual experience. You would not have had that visual experience if you weren't looking at a zebra. If you were looking at an elephant or that popcorn stand or something else around here, your visual experience would have been much different. But if you were looking at a cleverly painted mule, you would have had an experience just like the one you had when you were looking at that zebra. So your visual experience is a conclusive reason for believing that's a zebra but it's not a conclusive reason for believing that's not a cleverly painted mule. That's why you can know it's a zebra but you cannot know it's not a cleverly painted mule.

Conclusive Reasons

B: So conclusive reasons don't need to be entailing reasons.

F: Correct. Your visual experience doesn't logically entail that's a zebra in the sense that there are some possible worlds where you have that sort of visual experience but there is a cleverly painted mule in front of you. But, as we agreed earlier, those sorts of worlds are way far out.

B: Okay and so, in the nearby possible worlds, wherever I have that sort of experience, there is in fact a zebra in front of me.

F: Correct. In other words, the nearest non-zebra world is also a world where you aren't having that sort of experience but a different one. That's enough to make your visual experience a conclusive reason. Notice, however, that your visual experience is not a conclusive reason for thinking that's not a cleverly painted mule. If you were looking at a cleverly painted mule you would have had the same experience.

B: Okay. I get why you think I don't know it's not a cleverly painted mule even though I know it's a zebra. But, if I don't know it's not a cleverly painted mule, how can I know it's not a mule?

F: If you were looking at a mule, you wouldn't have had a visual experience like that. The only way you could've had that sort of visual experience and been looking at a mule is if you were looking at one of those cleverly painted mules. But, as we already agreed, cleverly painted mules are far out. That makes your visual experience a conclusive reason to believe that's not a mule.

B: So I know it's not a *mule* but I don't know it's not a *cleverly painted* mule.

F: Exactly. Since you examined the animal closely enough to know it's a zebra, you examined the animal closely enough to rule out it being a mule. But you can't rule out it being a cleverly painted mule because that would require gathering some additional evidence. Neither of us bothered to do that.

B: Do I also know it's not a member of the set of all mules?

F: Sure. After all, if there had been some member of the set of all mules in front of us, it wouldn't have been one of the cleverly painted mules. It would be one of the ordinary ones and in that case your visual experience would have been much different. So you know it's not a member of the set of all mules.

B: And if something is not a member of a given set, it is not a member of any subsets of that set. I know that's not a member of the set of all mules. And therefore I know it's not a member of any subset of the set of all mules. The set of all cleverly painted mules, of course, is one of the subsets of the set of all mules. But, for all I know, that is a member of the set of all cleverly painted mules.

F: Now you're speaking my language.

B: I also know it's not a mule that somebody put paint on but I don't know it's not a cleverly painted mule.

F: Come again?

B: The American Mule Racing Association often paints numbers on their mules for the races which I regularly attend and lay down a few bets. Had I been standing in front of a mule that somebody put paint on, it would have been one of those. And they're pretty sloppy about it. So, had I been standing in front of a mule that somebody put paint on, it wouldn't have been a *cleverly* painted mule and my visual experience would have been nothing like the one I had looking at that zebra. So I know that's not a mule that somebody put paint on. But I don't know it's not a cleverly painted mule.

F: If you say so.

B: And now that you mention it, I remember reading about how the Gaza City Zoo painted up a mule to look like a zebra.[11] I saw pictures and, I have to say, they did a pretty half-assed job.

F: They didn't paint the whole thing?

B: The black stripes weren't dark enough and, unlike zebra stripes, they were all of uniform width. To me, it didn't look anything like a zebra. It looked like a mule in faded prison garb. Even Earl Scheib would be embarrassed. The nearest possible world in which I was just standing in front of a mule that some

---

11 It was a donkey actually but you get the point. http://www.telegraph.co.uk/news/worldnews/middleeast/israel/6274874/Gaza-zookeepers-draw-crowds-with-painted-donkeys-after-zebras-die.html.

zoo officials painted in an effort to make it resemble a zebra is a world where I am at the Gaza City Zoo standing in front of their pathetic fake.

F: Uh, okay.

B: But my experience in that sort of situation would have been much different from the one I had looking at that zebra. Now of course someone cleverer than those guys could paint up a mule so that it looked just like a zebra even to me. In other words, I know that's not a mule that some zoo officials painted in an effort to make it resemble a zebra. But I don't know it's not a cleverly painted mule.

F: Right. Now before you go making any more sport of all this, don't forget that I never said these conjunctions are conversationally appropriate. I just said that they are true. Just like those instances of Moore's paradox.

B: Yeah, about that. I see why mooronic[12] conjunctions like "It's raining but I don't believe it" and "Dogs bark but I don't know it" are absurd things to say. I cannot assert either one because I cannot know either one. But according to you, frediculous conjunctions like "I know that's not a member of the set of all mules but I don't know it's not a cleverly painted mule" are knowable. Why not shout them from the rooftops?

F: Frediculous. That's cute. But let's be careful here. Although frediculous conjunctions are true, it's not clear to me that they are knowable. Consider this one: You know that's a zebra but you don't know it's not a cleverly painted mule. For the first conjunct to be true, you need to have conclusive reasons for believing that's a zebra. And you do. You wouldn't have had a visual experience like that had you not been looking at a zebra. The second conjunct is true because you do not have conclusive reasons for thinking that's not a cleverly painted mule. Had you been looking at a cleverly painted mule, your experience would have been the same.

B: Got it.

F: In order for you to know the conjunction *I know that's a zebra but I don't know it's not a cleverly painted mule*, you would have to know the first conjunct. Knowing the first conjunct amounts to *knowing that you know* that's a zebra. Knowing that one knows is a form of inoculation against skeptical

---

12 "Mooronic" is Laurence Goldstein's label for a Moore-paradoxical statement. For more, see his *Clear and Queer Thinking: Wittgenstein's Development and His Relevance to Modern Thought* (Lanham, MD: Rowan and Littlefield, 1999).

challenges.[13] You know that you know that's a zebra only if you know that your reasons for believing that's a zebra are conclusive.

B: Don't I know that my reasons are conclusive?

F: No. If you knew that your reasons were conclusive then you would be in a position to rule out that being a cleverly painted mule. And you aren't. Neither am I.

B: So knowing that P requires having conclusive reasons for P. But knowing that P does not require *knowing* that I have conclusive reasons for P. The reasons just have to be conclusive, whether I know they are or not. *Knowing that I know* that P, on the other hand, does require knowing that my reasons for P are conclusive.

F: Exactly. And thus you can know without being in any position to know that you know. Now, to generalize, frediculous conjunctions will be true only in cases where subjects lack second-order knowledge. "You know that's a zebra but you don't know that's not a cleverly painted mule" will be true only in cases where you don't know that you know that's a zebra. This is because knowing that you know that's a zebra entails knowing that your reasons are conclusive. So if you know that you know that's a zebra, then you *will* know that's not a cleverly painted mule. But this means that frediculous conjunctions will be true only when the subjects they concern do not know them to be true. This is why those conjunctions always sound so awful when we assert them.

> Does this commit Freddy to the Knowledge Account of Asserton?

B: Even though you've been asserting them all day.

F: Like I said before, good philosophy will always involve asserting inappropriate things. Why do you think they killed Socrates?

B: Something else is bothering me here, Freddie. I get that you think S knows that P only if S believes that P on the basis of R and R is a conclusive reason for P. What I'm not seeing is why you think knowing that I know that P requires knowing that R is a conclusive reason for P. Look at it this way. According to you, S knows that P whenever S has a true belief that P grounded upon a conclusive reason. Let S stand for me and let P stand for the proposition *I know that's a zebra*. Not the zoological proposition *that's a zebra* mind you, but the epistemic proposition *I know that's a zebra*. Your definition of knowledge entails that I cannot know the epistemic proposition unless I have conclusive reasons for it. The definition does not entail that I cannot know

---

13 Dretske says this in "Conclusive Reasons," *Australasian Journal of Philosophy* 49(1): 1–22, 17 (1971).

the epistemic proposition unless I know that I have conclusive reasons for the zoological proposition.

F: But you will have conclusive reasons for the epistemic proposition only if you know that your reasons for believing the zoological proposition are conclusive.

B: Why would that be? Take my actual situation. Suppose that my visual experience is my reason for believing not only *that's a zebra* but suppose also that, on the basis of that same experience, I believe *that I know* that's a zebra. It is natural to think I'd do this. Had I said "I know that's a zebra" and you asked "What makes you think you know that's a zebra?" I'd say "I'm looking right at it." My perceptual experience is grounds for believing both the zoological proposition and the epistemic one.

F: But your visual experience alone will not be a conclusive reason for believing that *you know* that's a zebra.

B: Why not? Let's apply the test. R is a conclusive reason for P if and only if R would not be the case unless P were the case. So, when we are wondering whether my experience constitutes conclusive reason to believe the proposition *I know that's a zebra*, the relevant question is this: Could I have had that experience had I not *known* that's a zebra? One way for me to fail to know that's a zebra is for it to be one of those cleverly painted mules. And, in that case, I will have the same experience I had when I was looking at that zebra. But of course, that is not the only way I can fail to know that's a zebra. And, as we agree, that is one of the more far out ways for me to fail to know that's a zebra. There are lots of other ways I might have failed to know that's a zebra. I might have failed to know that's a zebra if I hadn't bothered to come over here and look at it or, if the zookeeper had decided to give him the day off and keep him inside, or if I hadn't come to the zoo at all today, or if he had escaped his pen last night and wandered into the lion den and been eaten. All these ways I might have failed to know that's a zebra are much closer possibilities than the cleverly painted mule scenario. And notice that in each of these situations (and in every other plausible way of failing to know that's a zebra that I can think of), I do not have the sort of visual experience I had when I was looking at that zebra. This shows that if I had failed to know that's a zebra, I wouldn't have had that visual experience. I wouldn't have had that experience unless that *was* a zebra and I wouldn't have had it unless I *knew* that was a zebra. My visual experience is therefore a conclusive reason for believing that I know that's a zebra.

F: So you are saying that you can know that you know that's a zebra without knowing that your reasons for believing that's a zebra are conclusive.

B: That's what you say, Freddie. Or at least that's what your own view on the nature of knowledge says.

F: How's that?

B: Look at it this way. Earlier, you were assuming that the only way I could know that I know that's a zebra is to know that I have conclusive reasons for believing that's a zebra. Now that might be *one way* to know that I know but, given your own view on the nature of knowledge there's no reason why it should be the only way. As long as I have some reason R such that R would not be the case unless "I know that's a zebra" is true, then R is a conclusive reason for "I know that's a zebra" and I can on the basis of R know *that I know* that's a zebra.

F: And you think your perceptual experience, the same thing that serves as your reason for believing the zoological proposition, also fits the bill for being a conclusive reason for the epistemic one.

B: Yep.

F: Well I'm still not quite sure that your visual experience passes the test for being a conclusive reason for knowing that you know that's a zebra. Counterfactuals like this are a slippery and shifty business.[14] And some of what you said there kind of sounded like you might be guilty of backtracking.[15] I was thinking the same thing about some of the examples you were using earlier. In other words—Oh Look! There's a sign that says "MULE EXHIBIT THAT WAY" with an arrow pointing left. Let's go.

B: Of course, we don't know that the mule exhibit isn't somewhere else and the sign is wrong but we know the mule exhibit is over that way.

F: That's right, Betty. A signal can provide information but it cannot provide the information that it isn't misrepresenting things.

B: But if you look closely at the bottom of the sign you'll notice it says "AAAOK Zoo Signs, Inc. Your source for accurate zoo signage since 1976."

F: Uh huh.

> Is this true? If so, does it mean we can never know that sense perception accurately represents reality?

---

14 Dretske says this in his "Reply to Hawthorne," in *Contemporary Debates in Epistemology*, 44.
15 A man who hates his boss has a conversation with him where he pretends to like him. Immediately afterwards, he thinks to himself, "If I had said what I really think of my boss a minute ago, I would have been fired." False! He would never tell his boss what he thinks of him to his face. If he had said what he really thinks of his boss, his boss would not have been in the room. This is an example of backtracking. For a discussion see David Lewis, "Counterfactual Dependence and Time's Arrow," *Noûs* 13(4): 455–76 (1979).

The two begin to walk toward the mule exhibit.

B: Something else just occurred to me, Freddie. Take another look at the belief I arrived at back there at the zebra exhibit. I believed that the animal I was looking at was not a cleverly painted mule. You say I don't know this because my reason for believing it was my visual experience and I would have had that visual experience even if I had been looking at a cleverly painted mule.

F: That's right, Betty. Your reason for thinking that you were not looking at a cleverly painted mule is inconclusive.

B: But what's wrong with this? Suppose I say that my reason for believing that's not a cleverly painted mule is not my visual experience but my belief *that it's a zebra*. It certainly seems like I could believe *that's a zebra* and from there infer *that's not a cleverly painted mule*. In fact that's pretty much what I did back when we first started talking about this stuff. I formed a belief that that's not a cleverly painted mule via an argument whose key premise was *that's a zebra*. Now *that's a zebra* would not be true unless it were not a cleverly painted mule. In other words, if it were a cleverly painted mule, it wouldn't be a zebra. Therefore, *that's a zebra* is a conclusive reason for believing that it's not a cleverly painted mule.

F: Nice try, Betty. But look, your reason for believing *that's a zebra* is your visual experience. Right?

B: Yep.

F: If your visual experience is your reason for believing *that's a zebra* and *that's a zebra* is your reason for believing *that's not a cleverly painted mule*, then your visual experience is your reason for believing *that's not a cleverly painted mule*. And we've already agreed that your visual experience is not a conclusive reason for believing that's not a cleverly painted mule. Therefore, you do not have a conclusive reason to believe that's not a cleverly painted mule.

B: You are assuming that reasons are transitive. If R is a reason for P and P is a reason for Q then R is a reason for Q. Why not reject transitivity?

F: I do reject transitivity. I think your perceptual experience is a conclusive reason for believing that's a zebra. And if it's a zebra then it's not a cleverly painted mule. But your perceptual experience is not a conclusive reason for believing it's not a cleverly painted mule.

B: I'm not talking about the transitivity of conclusiveness. I am talking about the transitivity of reasons simpliciter or, if you prefer, the transitivity of the basing relation. I'm saying my basis for believing that's not a cleverly painted mule is that it's a zebra. And my basis for believing it's a zebra is my perceptual experience. But it follows that my basis for believing it's not a cleverly painted mule is my perceptual experience only if we assume that the basing relation is transitive. So why not reject that? Why not say that my reason for believing that's not a cleverly painted mule is just that it's a zebra and stop there? And look at what we gain if we do. We get a way to refute skepticism. Not only is *that's a zebra* a conclusive reason for *that's not a cleverly painted mule* but *I have hands* is a conclusive reason for *I am not a handless brain in a vat*. It would not be true that I have hands unless it were true that I am not a handless brain in a vat.

F: The Principle of the Transitivity of Reasons is an obvious epistemic principle, Betty. You can't go around denying obvious epistemic principles just because it gives you a nifty way to defeat skepticism.

B: Is that right?

F: That's right, Betty. And I know what you're smirking about but I don't deny closure just because it gives me a nifty way to defeat skepticism. I deny closure because of general facts about the nature of knowledge.[16]

B: But one of these "general facts about the nature of knowledge" is supposed to be the idea that knowledge requires conclusive reasons. This fact about knowledge does not get you a denial of closure. The most it shows is that either closure fails or reasons are not transitive.

F: Well I suppose that if you could give me some independent argument against the transitivity principle,[17] I might—Wow! There it is. Look at that mule. Beautiful.

B: It sure is, Freddie. It sure is.

---

16 Dretske, "Reply to Hawthorne," 43.
17 For such an argument, see John Post's "Infinite Regresses of Justification and Explanation," *Philosophical Studies* 38(1): 31–52 (1980).

The Paradox of the Preface
Philosophy Takes a Stand

Is it ever rational to be logically inconsistent? Even on purpose? An example from D.C. Mankinson convinces many that the answer is yes.[1] Suppose an expert historian has written a lengthy book. She has carefully checked each sentence in the manuscript and had some colleagues double-check it. Given this expert scrutiny, many will be happy to say it is rational for her to believe each sentence in the book and that she knows each sentence in the book. But, on the other hand, she is well aware that she is a fallible human being, the book is long, and parts of it are controversial. So, the thought goes, it is also rational for her to believe that there is at least one false statement in there somewhere. Everybody makes mistakes. So she writes a preface to the book that says something like this: "Although I have carefully checked each sentence in this book, this book is sure to contain mistakes. The errors are all my own." If we take the author at her word, we are forced to say that she believes that each sentence in the book is true and she also believes that one of the sentences in the book is false. And that is logically inconsistent. Yet, many say this is exactly what she should believe; it is rational for her to be inconsistent. This is what has come to be known as the paradox of the preface.

Alan Goldman offers the following variation.

> Suppose A has to total 500 sets of figures and does so by the usual method of non-machine-aided addition. If all his totals turn out

---

[1] David C. Mankinson, "The Paradox of the Preface," *Analysis* 25(6): 205–07 (1965).

correct, we have no hesitation in saying he knows each since his method of arriving at belief was reliable and hence justificatory. But given that the average totaler, which A is, makes 1 error for every 200 additions, it would not be rational for him to believe that he has made no error, that all his totals are real sums.[2]

Here again someone believes each member of a set of statements—considered individually—but also believes that one of those statements is false. That is inconsistent. But, according to Goldman, this is the rational attitude to take.

The idea is interesting all by itself. But it also has interesting consequences. Anyone who thinks these examples constitute cases where it is rational to be knowingly inconsistent, must deny that knowledge is closed under known entailment. But the reason for denying closure in this case is different from the reason discussed in the last chapter. The deductions involved are also much longer.

Consider again the historian's book. Let's call the first sentence in the book S1, the second S2, and so on up to Sn which is the last sentence of the book. Now imagine an argument where each premise is a sentence of the book and the conclusion is just the conjunction of those premises. In other words:

1. S1
2. S2
...
n. Sn
_____
n+1. Therefore, (S1 & S2 ... & Sn)

This argument is an instance of a valid rule; any set of individual statements logically entails the conjunction of those statements. If what is said above is correct, the historian can know each premise of this argument. But it is not rational for her to believe the conclusion even though she knows the argument is valid. In fact, it is rational for her to believe that the conclusion is *false* even though she knows the argument is valid and knows that each of the premises is true. Something similar can be said of the person who calculates sums in Goldman's example.

The kind of closure denial in play here concerns arguments that contain a large number of premises. Many epistemologists would agree with Betty's

---

2 Alan H. Goldman, "A Note on the Conjunctivity of Knowledge," *Analysis* 36(1): 5–9 (1975).

suggestion in the previous chapter that the kind of closure denial Freddie advocates is implausible but still find this multi-premise variety rather appealing.[3]

The general idea here can be extended from the historian's book and Goldman's list of sums to your own mind. For each thing you believe, you believe that it is true. But you should also believe that something you believe is false. Nobody's perfect. So it is rational for you to be logically inconsistent.

Another paradox that appears in this chapter is the sorites or heap paradox. Consider the following argument.

1. 1 grain of sand does not make a heap.
2. For any n, if n grains of sand do not make a heap, then n+1 grains of sand do not make a heap.

---

3. Therefore, 10 million grains of sand do not make a heap.

The first premise looks obviously true, the conclusion looks obviously false. The second, or "inductive" step, just says that you cannot transform something that is not a heap of sand into a heap of sand by adding a single grain. To deny the second premise would be to say that there is a precise cut-off point somewhere, that there is a specific number of grains of sand for which that many grains is a heap and yet one grain less is not. But how could that be?

The same kind of argument can be constructed for terms like "rich" (1. Someone with only one penny is not rich, ...), "tall" (1. Someone with a height of one inch is not tall, ...), and many others. The sorites paradox brings out the philosophical problems inherent in the phenomenon of vagueness.

One school of the thought says that the second premise is false. There is a precise cut off point for all vague terms. But, the thought goes, we do not and cannot know where it is. This is known as the epistemic view of vagueness.[4]

In this dialogue, a philosopher who believes in rationally inconsistent beliefs (and the epistemic view of vagueness) takes the witness stand in a court case where he is grilled by a prosecutor. Some of the themes from the last chapter are explored in more detail as are some new issues.

TV Announcer: Thank you for tuning in for another action-packed hour of real life courtroom drama. Let's watch as our Defendant is sworn in.

Bailiff: State your name.

---

3 For a discussion of single- versus multi-premise closure denial, see John Hawthorne, *Knowledge and Lotteries* (Oxford: Oxford UP, 2003).
4 For more on the sorites paradox, see Dominic Hyde's entry "Sorites Paradox," in *The Stanford Encyclopedia of Philosophy* https://plato.stanford.edu/entries/sorites-paradox/.

Defendant: Bertrand Immanuel van Kripgenquine.

B: Occupation? I'm thinking philosopher.

D: You know it.

B: Religion?

D: Anomalous Monist.

B: Anolamawama-who? Well, we all believe in Him in our own way.[5]

D: But not everybody believes in just *one* type of thing.

B: Just one thing? That is weird.

D: Anomalous. And type of thing.

B: Whatever. Do you swear to tell the truth, the whole truth, and nothing but the truth?

D: Depends.

Prosecutor: It *depends*? Your Honor, this is an outrage!

Judge: I'll allow it—provided the witness can explain.

D: Well, like I said, it depends.

J: I'll need to know what it depends on. But before you tell me, I notice you have chosen to represent yourself.

D: That's right.

J: Are you aware that anyone who represents himself in a court of law has a fool for a client?

D: Are you aware that anyone who doesn't has an overpaid crook for an attorney?

J: On what does your telling the truth depend?

D: It depends on how long I'll be talking. You think I'll be up here a while?

J: Oh yes. This case is very complicated and there will be many questions.

---

5   Here is how Bertrand Russell described his experience upon checking into prison during World War I: "I was much cheered, on my arrival, by the warder at the gate, who had to take particulars about me. He asked my religion and I replied 'agnostic.' He asked me how to spell it and remarked with a sigh: 'Well, there are many religions, but I suppose they all worship the same God.'" *The Autobiography of Bertrand Russell 1914–1944* (Boston: Little, Brown and Company, 1951), 30.

D: Then you can bet I'll say something false.

P: Your Honor, the witness has preconfessed to perjury! I move that he be charged and—

D: Whoa. Perjury happens when somebody *intentionally* says something false. I don't plan on doing that.

J: Then why not take the oath?

D: Because that's not what the oath says. I can swear that I'll *believe* what I say. I can even swear to the truth of each *particular* thing I say. But I can't swear to the truth of *all* of what I say.

J: Not sure I understand that. Why can't you swear to all of it?

D: The longer I talk, the more I'll say and thus the more likely it'll be that I'll say something false. And so if I'm going to be up here a long time testifying to various minute details of the case, then I'm bound to say something that's not true. I mean, I'm only human. We all make mistakes.

P: Is it common for you to make mistakes?

D: If you're asking whether I've ever committed the fallacy of denying the antecedent, then the answer is no.

P: I'm not asking that.

D: Well then I gotta say yes.

P: What?

J: Here's what I don't understand, sir. You've already said you will not willingly say anything false.

D: That's correct. In fact, Your Honor, I can go you even better than that. For each particular thing I say, I am prepared to swear that it is true.

J: Okay. You are prepared to swear that everything you say will be true. Do that so we can proceed.

D: Not so fast, Your Honor. There's a big difference between swearing to the truth of a set of statements individually—*one by one* as it were—and swearing to the truth of the whole thing.

J: Come again?

D: Suppose somebody writes a history book. And not just anybody. Suppose it's a big-time history professor. He writes this long and ambitious book. Some of what he says is controversial. Gotta keep it interesting!

J: But it is still a *history* book.

D: Yeah so there's a limit. Anyway, this guy's a very meticulous scholar and he's gone over every word of the thing dozens of times. He's not going to put anything in there unless he's convinced it's absolutely true. He even has a couple colleagues give it the same treatment. At the end of this process, he goes through his book page by page and points to each sentence, mulls it over a bit and says, "Yep. That's true." But he's aware that he's a fallible human being. And he knows that every other book he's ever read had mistakes in it. It would be a miracle if his book didn't too. So he writes a preface that says something like this, "I thank Professors X, Y, and Z, for helping me scrutinize this work. Nonetheless, this book is sure to contain some mistakes. The errors are all my own." In other words, even though he's convinced of the truth of each sentence in the book, he thinks there's gotta be a falsehood in there somewhere. And it is rational for him to think that. How could the book not contain a mistake?

P: Why would the errors be "all his own"? Other people looked at it too. Seems like they deserve some of the blame. And doesn't the guy have an editor? What kind of press is this?

D: Of course the guy blames everybody else for the mistakes. He's a professor. But that part's just kinda something you say. The point is—

P: Your Honor, as entertaining as all of this is, I do think we should proceed with the trial. If the witness will not take the oath then—

J: No, I'll allow it. I think I see where this is going. So you are saying that although the author rationally believes each sentence in his book, it is also rational for him to believe that something in there is false.

P: Your Honor, I object. It can't be rational to believe a contradiction. I refer you to the case of *Hegel versus*—

D: No one's believing a contradiction here, Your Honor. To believe a contradiction is to believe something of the form *P and Not-P*. That's not what the author is doing.

P: He believes everything in the book and yet he believes that something in there is false. Contradiction.

D: You're not getting it. Think of it this way. Suppose the book is n sentences long.

P: How long?

D: n.

P: n?

D: Yeah. n is number.

P: Since when is n a number?

D: Okay. Let n be a number.

P: How do I let a letter be a number? For that matter, how do I *let* anything be a number? Can I stop something from being a number? Your Honor, I must strenuously object to this insult to the integrity of the English lang—

J: Counsel will let n be number. Proceed, sir.

D: Call the first sentence in the book S1, the second S2 and so on. The author believes that S1 is true, that S2 is true, that S3 is true dot dot dot all the way up to Sn which is the last sentence of the book. He also believes that at least one of those is false. In other words, he believes a long disjunction. Either S1 is false or S2 is false or S3 is false and so on.

P: But that long disjunction is equivalent to a negated conjunction. It's not the case that: S1 is true *and* S2 is true *and* dot dot dot on up to Sn.

D: Yeah, so?

P: So since he's checked each sentence in the book, he believes the conjunction—S1 is true *and* S2 is true and so on. But you just said he also believes the negation of that conjunction. There's your contradiction.

D: Except he doesn't believe the conjunction of everything in his book. That's what I've been trying to tell you. He believes each statement of his book *considered individually* but that's different from believing the conjunction of every statement in his book. It's one thing to believe S1, to believe S2, to believe S3, and so forth. It's quite another to believe the conjunction: S1 *and* S2 *and* S3 *and* et cetera.

P: How can you believe a bunch of statements individually without believing their conjunction?

D: It happens all the time, especially if it's explicit conscious belief we're talking about here. I mean you believe each thing you believe. No denying that. But to believe the proposition that is the conjunction of everything you believe, well that'd be one enormous proposition. You couldn't even get your mind around something like that. Much less write it down. So what's going on with our author and his book is the same thing on a smaller scale. Now in this case, I guess he could explicitly believe the conjunction of everything in the book if he's really smart. Or I suppose he could just hold up the book and say "everything in here is true." But he wisely declines to do that. It would be irrational to believe everything in the book is true. All books say some false things. Everybody knows that.

J: So the idea is that the author believes each statement in his book.

D: Considered individually, yes.

J: And he also believes something in the book is false. In other words, he believes the negation of the conjunction of each statement in his book. But, since he refuses to believe the conjunction of everything in the book, we needn't say he believes a contradiction.

D: You got it. In a sense, he doesn't even have contradictory beliefs. Since he does not believe the conjunction of everything in his book, there are no two of his beliefs that contradict one another. No particular thing he says in the book entails that any other particular thing he says in there is false—even if you include the preface.

J: Okay, no pair of contradictory beliefs and no belief in a contradiction. So the case of *Hegel versus Wisdom* has no relevance.

P: But Your Honor, even if no two of the sentences in the book are inconsistent, *the book* is inconsistent—if we include the preface. There's no way around that.

D: He's right, Your Honor. But that's what I've been trying to say all along. This is a case where it is rational to say and believe inconsistent things.

P: But if the book is inconsistent then it couldn't possibly be true, Your Honor—exactly what the court found in *Hegel*. What difference does it make if what the author says is merely inconsistent rather than "contradictory" in some strict sense?

D: It makes a big difference. If I identify some particular proposition as contradictory then I know that it cannot be true. That's why I can't get myself to believe it. And once I identify a pair of my beliefs as inconsistent then I know that one of the two is false. So I've got to give them both up until I can sort out which one's the joker. Now our author, he believes each sentence in a very long book and he believes that at least one of those is false. But he can't narrow it down beyond that. It's not at all like believing a contradiction or having a pair of contradictory beliefs.

P: I still want to know what this has to do with our trial.

D: Oh, I can answer that. Just as it is rational for our author to expect something he says in his book to be false, it is rational for me to believe that something I say up here will be false—provided I testify for long enough. But, like our author, I'm willing to swear that each particular assertion I make up here is true. If you like, I can take the oath, answer one question, take it again, answer another question, and so forth. That way I am only swearing to the truth of each *individual* thing I say and not the truth of *every*—

P: Objection, Your Honor. That would be an unnecessary waste of the Court's time. I give you Exhibit A.

D: Exhibit A? Is the trial starting? I haven't even taken the oath.

J: I'll allow it.

P: As you can see, this is a long list of arithmetic equations.

J: Bailiff?

Goldman's Variation on the Preface

B: Looks like math to me, Your Honor.

P: Now I ask the Defendant. What is the status of the equations found here?

D: The status?

P: Yes. Are they all true? All false? Some true and some false?

D: How should I know? I can't see it from here. Heck, for all I know, that list was written by Richard Feynman or it just says 1 plus 1 equals 2 over and over again—in which case they're all true. Or maybe the equations were produced randomly. And in that case I bet it's full of falsehoods. I really have no clue.

P: With the court's permission, I ask you to go through and check each equation.

D: Objection, Your Honor. No one told me there was going to be a quiz.

J: I'll allow it. The Court will adjourn for recess while the Defendant performs these calculations.

D: Math at recess? Your Honor I object. There's no math at recess! This is highly irregular.

J: So's Your Honor—another reason for a recess. Overruled.

After recess, things resume.

P: Did you check the equations for accuracy?

D: Yes.

P: Is the first equation on the list true?

D: Yes.

P: And the second?

D: Yes.

P: And the third?

J: Counselor, where are we going with this?

P: Your Honor, if you'll humor me for just a minute. I mean, I did sit through all that stuff about the history book.

D: Well I certainly have no idea where he's going, Your Honor, but perhaps I can speed things up. I checked each equation on the list. I found each one to be true. So no need to ask me about them one by one. I am going to say that each one is true.

P: Do you consider yourself to be reliable at arithmetic calculations?

D: Oh yes. Very. I'd estimate my reliability for this level of math to be right around 99 per cent.

P: And would you say that your calculations here were careful?

D: Would and will. My calculations were very careful even though I was supposed to be at recess.

P: So you are prepared to testify that every equation on this list is true?

D: Nope. Quite the contrary. I have very good reason to believe that at least one of them is false.

P: You do? Will you please explain to the court why that is?

D: It's a matter of probabilities. I checked the first equation on the list and found it to be true. As I said, I'm a very reliable calculator of arithmetic equations—not perfect but good enough to know. And I did the same for the second one, and each of the others. So I'm happy to say of each equation on the list that it is true. But in order for me to know that *all* of the equations on the list are true, it would have to be that I performed the first calculation correctly *and* I performed the second one correctly *and* so on for all the rest. But the probability of all that happening is really low. In fact, given the length of that list, it is overwhelmingly likely that I made a mistake in there somewhere.

P: But isn't it true, Mr. van Kripgenquine, that you are at least 99 per cent reliable at calculating simple sums like this?

D: Absolutely.

P: So shouldn't we think there's only a miniscule chance you made a mistake?

D: No not at all. This is just elementary probability theory. You see, since I'm a 99 per cent reliable mathematician, there's a 99 per cent probability that I performed the first calculation correctly. And there's a 99 per cent probability that I performed the second calculation correctly. And so on for each one. Now, again, to say that I performed *all* of the calculations correctly is to say that I performed the first correctly *and* I performed the second correctly *and* dot dot dot all the way down the list. But the probability of a conjunction of independent events all coming about is the *product* of the probability of each one coming about. In other words, the probability that I performed *all* the calculations correctly will be point 99 times point 99 times point 99 and so on for however many equations there are on that list. And that's well over 200. So it is overwhelmingly likely I made a mistake somewhere. So it would be irrational for me to believe that all the equations on that list are true. Given how many equations you've got here, it's pretty much certain that I made a mistake and one of them is false.[6] So that's what I believe. At least one of them is false. This is exactly what I said about the book preface and about my own testimony all over again. I don't see why you had to ruin recess like that.

J: He's right. We've been over this. What's the point?

P: Your Honor, I'd like to refer you back to what the witness said regarding the list before he performed his calculations.

J: Shall I have the stenographer read it?

D: No need, Your Honor. He asked what the status of the equations on this list was and I said I did not know.

P: That's correct. You said you didn't know whether they were all true, all false, or some true and some false. Why did you say that?

D: Because I had no reason to think anything one way or the other at the time.

P: And how do you answer that question now?

---

6 If there are 200 equations, it's around 99.87 per cent.

D: Which question?

P: The question about the status of the list. Is everything it says true, everything false, or a bit of both?

D: Well, like I said, it's got to be that at least one of the equations on that list is false.

P: So your position has changed. You went from having no idea whether the list contains a falsehood to being quite sure there's a falsehood on there somewhere. Is that true?

D: Yes. I am now as sure as a philosopher can be that there's a falsehood on there somewhere.

P: And what brought about your change of mind? What good reason do you now have to think something on the list is false that you did not have before recess?

D: My calculations.

P: And what was the result of your calculations?

D: Like I said, I found that each equation is true.

P: So you went from having no reason at all to believe the list contained a falsehood to having a very strong reason to think there's a falsehood there—the reason being that you carefully checked each equation *and found it to be true.*

D: That's right.

P: This is what I'm trying to say here, Your Honor. The defendant's position is absurd.

J: How so?

P: Did you hear what he just said?

J: Yes. But why is it absurd?

> Given what he has said so far, does the Defendant have to say this about these examples? Is the Prosecutor correct to think there is an absurdity here?

P: Because that's the opposite of how inquiry works. "Are the statements found here all true?" "Well, gee whiz lemme check. The first one's true. The second one's true and so on for each of the rest. So, nope one of 'ems gotta be false!" Or how 'bout this? "We're worried about those hundreds of cats in that beat-up house down the road there, Mr. Animal Control Officer. Are any of them rabid?" "Well we tested each of the cats for rabies and each one came back negative for rabies. So, yes, one of those cats has rabies." Or what if—

J: The Court sees your point, Counselor. This consequence of the Defendant's position is a bit odd. But what's the relevance?

P: The same reasoning is what drove the Defendant to say that stuff about the preface and about his testimony before the Court, Your Honor. I've shown it's absurd.

J: There's a difference. The Defendant's chief reason for thinking the list contains a falsehood is that he's 99 per cent reliable and he found each to be true. But the history professor's reason for thinking his book contains a falsehood is not that he checked each sentence and found it to be true. It's an inductive argument from past experience—every book he's run across said something false, so his will too. Ditto for the Defendant's reason for thinking that his testimony would contain a falsehood. Everybody says something false if he talks for long enough.

P: I'd like to address that too, Your Honor. There is a general background of inductive evidence that provides the author with a kind of *indirect* basis for thinking that his book contains a falsehood. But, once the author checks each sentence in the book and has a few colleagues give it the once over too, he has *direct* evidence for the veracity of each statement in the book. This provides *deductive* support for the claim that everything in the book is true. Direct deductive evidence versus indirect inductive evidence. Everybody knows who wins that one.

D: He's missing my point again, Your Honor. He thinks that since they've found each sentence to be true, it's reasonable for them to conclude they're all true. But the fact that every other book the author has run across contains a falsehood serves as an *epistemic defeater* for that.

J: A what now?

D: A defeater. For example, suppose you have good reason to believe your favorite TV show is coming on at 8.

J: *Murder, She Wrote!*

D: Uh, yeah. So you've watched a lot of *Murder, She Wrote* and that's when it's always come on in the past. But then you get news that the President is going to make a special speech at 8 and it will be aired on all the channels. That news *defeats* the support you had for believing *Murder, She Wrote* would come on at 8.

J: Thanks a lot, Trump.

> Evidence *E* serves as a *rebutting* defeater for your belief that *P* when *E* is evidence that *P* is false. *E* is an *undermining* defeater for your belief that *P* when *E* is evidence that your basis for believing *P* is weak.

D: You might think the fact this guy has checked every sentence in the book gives him a reason to believe that everything in the book is true. But this other fact, the fact that every other book the guy's read said some false things is a defeater. It doesn't defeat any particular statement in the book because the background evidence doesn't identify any particular thing as mistaken. But it defeats the rationality of the inference from the claim that each particular statement is true to the claim that all of them are true. As I keep repeating, all books make mistakes. Since you've done such careful checking, you can rationally believe each statement in the book. But you cannot draw the inference that everything in the book is true because that inference is defeated by your background evidence.

Which sort of defeater is the Defendant referring to?

P: Objection! Since when is a deductively valid inference defeasible? If you have what you know is a deductively valid inference, and you rationally believe each premise, you can get evidence that undermines a premise or maybe get evidence that undermines your belief in the validity of the inference but you can't get evidence that undermines the inference without doing either of those. Deduction doesn't work like that.

Who is correct here, the Prosecutor or the Defendant?

D: Does too.

P: Furthermore, in the case of what's on TV, there is no deductively valid inference from your belief that *Murder, She Wrote*'s been on at 8 every night in the past to the conclusion that it will start at 8 tonight. That's induction not deduction. The case of the history book is different. If each sentence in the book is true, there's no possible way they couldn't all be. So there is a deductively valid inference from each sentence in the book to the conjunction of them. That means the direction of defeat goes the other way. The inductive evidence for there being a falsehood in the book gets undermined once we carefully check each sentence in the book—especially since the inductive argument is based on *other* books and thus bears only *indirectly* on what's in this book.

J: So if I used deduction that would mean the President couldn't cancel *Murder, She Wrote*?

P: Uhh, I don't think so. But what do I know? To quote your favorite show, "I'm just a simple southern lawyah."

D: Objection, Your Honor! The Prosecutor is thoroughly confused. He doesn't even know Andy from Angela. And if he's right, then why do so many books have prefaces that say something in the book is false?

P: I'd like to answer that, Your Honor. The defendant has already admitted that the line about "the mistakes here are all my own" isn't sincere. It's just something you say to sound polite. I think the stuff about there being mistakes in the book is also just something you say. Nobody likes a know-it-all. Notice also that these prefaces never say "this book contains errors." Instead they say things like "this book is sure to contain errors." The "is sure to" stuff is not indicating an attitude of certainty or even belief. Quite the opposite. It's indicating that the author doesn't really have any direct evidence for thinking there's a mistake in there. It's a little like strolling into a bar and saying "Does anybody have a light? Surely, somebody in here's a smoker." That's a way of saying you don't really know or even necessarily believe that somebody's a smoker, you just think it might be a good guess.[7]

> Is it plausible to think terms like "surely," "certainly," or "it's gotta be that" can signal an attitude of *uncertainty*?

J: Call me Shirley again and I'll never lend you my lighter.

P: Good one, Your Honor. And another thing. Is it true that every book contains a falsehood? He keeps saying that but has anyone ever checked it out? You read books, often you disagree with what's in there. But how do you get from there to some sort of rock solid fact that every book contains a falsehood? Even one you wrote and double-checked yourself! What grounds do we really have for that attitude, Your Honor?

D: I've read alotta books and all of them contained at least one falsehood.

P: And how do you know that?

D: What do you mean?

P: Did the first book you read contain a falsehood?

D: Yes.

P: And the second?

D: Yes.

P: And each of the others?

D: You know it.

P: So you have a long list of books you've read. You find that each one contains a falsehood. And from that you conclude that all the books you've read contain a falsehood.

D: Naturally.

Bailiff: Gotcha!

D: How is that a gotcha? And why is the Bailiff testifying?

---

[7] Brian Kim uses this kind of point as the basis for an alternative solution to the preface paradox in "Surely This Paper Contains Some Errors," *Philosophical Studies* 172(4): 1013–29 (2015).

J: I'll allow it. Please explain, Bailiff.

B: Given everything else this fella's said, he should think at least one of the books he's read *didn't* contain a falsehood.

J: Why's that?

B: It's a matter of probabilities, Your Honor. Nothing's 100 per cent certain. So it isn't a hundred per cent certain there was a falsehood in that first book he read. But it's close enough to know. Call it 99 per cent. And it's 99 per cent that the second book contained a falsehood. Now if your reason for thinking every book contains a falsehood is gonna be any good at all, you better read a lotta books on a lotta unrelated subjects. But if you do that, the probability that every book you've read contained a falsehood will be the product of the probability that each did. Point 99 times point 99 times point 99 and so on. But then what you get is a really low number. And if you reason the way he does, you should think you musta made a mistake in there somewhere. So he should think at least one of the books he's read was nothing but the truth.

P: My point exactly, Your Honor. In the ideal case, he's got a big long list of books for which he's confirmed that each one has a falsehood in it. I still say he's never actually done that and neither has anybody else, but I'll let that slide for now. You've come to believe that each book on this list says something false. Now, by the defendant's own line of reasoning, he can't say *every* book contains a falsehood, he can't even say *every book he's read* contains a falsehood. In fact, he should say exactly the opposite. And then his whole argument falls apart.

D: Okay I'll give you that one of the books I've read contains no falsehoods. But I still maintain my theory that all books contain falsehoods. The one book that doesn't contain a falsehood is like Hume's missing shade of blue—it's the exception that proves the rule.[8]

J: The exception that proves the rule?

D: Yes. In other words, that there is one book my vast library that is nothing but the truth only helps support the general view that there is no book without a falsehood. The one all true book is the exception that proves the rule.

P: Your Honor, I strenuously object to exceptions proving rules. A counterexample can never be used to *support* a theory!

---

8   David Hume said that a person could form an idea of a shade of blue he had never seen if he had seen all the other shades of blue. This runs counter to Hume's own theory of the mind but he did not seem to regard that as a serious problem. For more, see Section 2 of David Hume, *An Enquiry Concerning Human Understanding* (Indianapolis: Hackett, 1993).

D: I agree wholeheartedly, Your Honor. A counterexample can never be used to support a theory. "The exception that proves the rule" being the exception that proves the rule.

J: What?

D: You can't expect me to give up on my theory that all books contain falsehoods just because of a single counterexample. No one has ever abandoned a theory because of just one counterexample.

P: That's not true. What about Gettier and the JTB theory? Didn't he give up the theory because of just one counterexample?

D: Yes. Gettier gave up a theory because of one counterexample. But no one has ever abandoned a theory because of just one counterexample.

J: What?

B: Didn't Gettier have two?[9]

D: Anyway, Your Honor, I don't need to say that every book contains a falsehood. Sure I said that but I was being colorful; after all, I'm not yet under oath. If I have a sample of books and I've confirmed that each one contains a falsehood, all I need to say is that the next one will too. The author of the history book can do the same. He can set up a long inductive argument whose premises cover a bunch of books he's read. The first premise says Book 1 contains a falsehood. The second premise says Book 2 contains a falsehood. And so on. Now for the conclusion, we don't need the generalization that all books contain falsehoods, just the singular claim that this book right here—the one he wrote—does.

P: Well I still say directly confirming that each sentence in the book is true and then making a deductively valid inference to the conclusion that all of them are true defeats the indirect inductive evidence regardless of how you construe that evidence or the conclusion you draw from it, Your Honor. But I want to move on to something else. I'm glad we've brought up arguments. I now introduce Exhibit B. This is the long list of arithmetic equations—Exhibit A—transformed into an argument.

> What considerations might settle this disagreement about the direction of defeat?

J: Transformed into an argument?

---

9 Yes. See Edmund Gettier, "Is Justified True Belief Knowledge?," *Analysis* 23: 121–23 (1963). The Gettier Problem will be discussed in a later chapter.

P: Yes. As you can see, I've taken each equation from the list I brought out earlier and made it into a premise of the argument. The conclusion of the argument is just the conjunction of each of those premises.

J: So it's one big conjunction introduction. Each premise is one of the equations from the list. And the conclusion is just the conjunction of those.

P: Exactly. Call the first equation on the list E1, the second E2 and so on up to the last equation on the list. We'll just call that En—assuming we're still letting letters be numbers. The first premise of the argument is just E1, the second is E2 and so on all the way down. The conclusion of the argument is the conjunction: E1 *and* E2 *and* dot dot dot En. Now I'd like to ask the defendant about this argument. Is the first premise of this argument true?

D: Since this is just the list put as an argument, I've already answered that. Yes. The first premise is true. And the second premise is true. And the third one. If he is just going to keep asking the same questions over and over, Your Honor—

J: I'll allow it. But please speed things up here.

P: Okay. So I was going to ask him whether the conclusion of this argument—which is just the conjunction of each of the premises—is true. But we know his answer. Since he thinks there's a falsehood lurking somewhere on the list, he rejects that big conjunction. So he thinks the conclusion of this argument is false. Now here's what I want to ask. Is this a valid argument?

D: Yes. It's just and-introduction. So it's valid.

P: And each of the premises is true?

D: Considered individually yes. Already said that. Several times.

P: So we have a valid argument, each of its premises is true but its conclusion is....?

D: False.

Multi-Premise Closure Denial

B: Gotcha!

P: Gotcha indeed, Your Honor. A valid argument with true premises can't have a false conclusion. Everybody knows that.

D: That's no gotcha. This is just a case where a subject (me) is rationally justified in believing the premises of an argument, knows that the argument is valid but isn't rational in believing the conclusion. The prosecution is assuming some sort of epistemic closure principle here. I reject that. That ought to be obvious from what I've been saying all along. I refer you to the case of *Dretske versus—*

P: *Dretske* has no relevance here, Your Honor. You will recall in that case the issue was whether a subject could know or rationally believe the premises of an argument, know that the argument is valid but fail to know or rationally believe the conclusion. But the defendant's position here is that each premise of this argument is true and the argument is valid but the conclusion is *false*. The findings in *Dretske* were pretty bad. A travesty I'd say. But this is far, far worse. Furthermore, the reasons for thinking the history book contains a falsehood or that the Defendant made a mistake in his calculations are not conclusive reasons in the sense defined in *Dretske*. If there were no falsehood in the book, the historian would still believe that there is. If the defendant hadn't said something false, he would still think he has.

> Can any inductive argument provide conclusive reasons in Dretske's sense?

J: Perhaps he shouldn't say that each premise of Exhibit B is true. What if he just went down your argument there, pointed to each premise and said "That's true"? And then pointed to the conclusion and said "That's false"? That way, he's asserting the truth of each premise but he isn't asserting the sentence "each premise is true."

P: Are you directing the witness, Your Honor?

J: I'll allow it.

P: These distinctions between knowing each and knowing all or asserting each one and asserting the sentence "each one is true" are not only phony but they are also red herrings. We can do the same thing with the history book. We can turn that into a great big case of conjunction introduction where each premise is one of the sentences in the book and the conclusion is a conjunction of those. If the author takes this guy's advice he's stuck saying the same silly things about that argument.

D: Your Honor, my whole point here has been that it can be rational to hold inconsistent beliefs. So what if I say the premises are each true and it's valid but the conclusion is false? Sometimes you have to be inconsistent.

P: See? You get comfortable with one sort of inconsistency and next thing you know you are saying inconsistent things about *arguments*. I won't even bother to ask whether he thinks the argument is sound. It's valid and its premises are each true. That makes it sound. And a sound argument cannot have a false conclusion. Yet, according to him, this one does. Nonsense. And I thought philosophers loved their logic above all else. I would have expected the children of Socrates to have more respect for reason than this.

D: Socrates was a terrible father, Your Honor. Just read the *Crito*.

P: If the Court will allow it, I'd like to introduce something else here. I give you Exhibit C. This is a simple two premise argument. The first premise is the first equation from the list, the second premise is the second equation from the list, and the conclusion is just the conjunction of those two. E1, E2, therefore, E1 *and* E2.

J: Got it. Proceed.

P: I ask the Defendant, is the first premise of this argument true?

D: I already answered that. Twice. The first premise is true. And so is the second. And in this case, I'm happy to say the conclusion is true too. My position is not that you can *never* know a conjunction by inferring it from its conjuncts. It's that you can rationally believe and even know a set of propositions individually and yet still not know their conjunction. But this will only happen if the set of propositions is really big or if each member of the set is only slightly above the threshold for rational belief.

J: The threshold?

D: Yes. For it to be rational to believe that P there's gotta be something that makes P likely to be true. How likely is likely enough? I can't give you any exact number and it may even move around with context. But that's not too important right now. My point is just that as long as the threshold for rational belief is below the level of 100 per cent certainty, you are going to have cases where it's rational to believe a set of propositions individually but it's not rational to believe their conjunction. This can happen if the set is really big. But it can also happen with small sets where the propositions are just at or barely above the threshold.

J: How so?

D: Suppose a belief that P is rational only if the subject's evidence allows him to be 90 per cent sure that P is true. If you have two independent propositions toward which the subject is 90 per cent confident, then—assuming degrees of rational confidence work the way probabilities do—the subject can only be 81 per cent confident in their conjunction. Point nine times point nine is point eight one. And that is below the threshold. So it's rational for our subject to believe each of these propositions but not their conjunction. In this case, it's because the propositions are right at the threshold—rationally believable but just barely. The same thing can happen with propositions well above the threshold if you have enough of them. That's what happens with the history book and with the list and my own testimony if we ever get to it. Now in the

> Some think closure denial is plausible if restricted to arguments with lots of premises. The Defendant's position on the preface paradox here leads him to the view that closure can fail in a two premise argument. Is there a way to deny closure for very long arguments without having to deny it for at least some simple two premise arguments?

case he just gave me, Exhibit C there, we've got two simple arithmetic equations. Wherever the threshold is, my rational confidence in these is well above it. So I don't see any real risk in inferring that the conjunction of them is true.

J: Got it.

P: Great. Now I introduce Exhibit D, Your Honor, an argument whose premises are the first three equations on the list and the conclusion is the conjunction of those. E1, E2, E3; therefore E1 *and* E2 *and* E3. Also, I give you Exhibit E which is an argument whose premises are the first four equations on the list and the conclusion is the conjunction of those. And now I introduce Exhibit F. This is an argument whose premises are the first five equations on the list and—

J: How many exhibits do you have here, Counselor?

P: A whole bunch, Your Honor. You see, I made a series of arguments. All of them are examples of conjunction introduction. The first in the series is Exhibit C—that's the one where the premises are the first two equations on the list and the conclusion is the conjunction of those. E1, E2; therefore E1 *and* E2. Then we have Exhibit D which, as I said, goes E1, E2, E3; therefore, E1 *and* E2 *and* E3. Exhibit E goes E1, E2, E3, E4; therefore E1 *and* E2 *and* E3 *and* E4. And the series continues like this until we have an argument whose premises consist of each equation on the list and the conclusion is the conjunction of all those. That was Exhibit B if you recall—Exhibit A being the list itself.

J: Neat. But what's the point? Why did you bother assembling all of these arguments?

D: Because he bills by the hour?

P: According to Mr. van Kripgenquine, each of Exhibit B's premises are true but the conclusion is false—even though it's a valid argument. I've already said what I think about that. He says each of Exhibit C's premises are true. But there he's willing to say that conclusion is true too because the conclusion is still well above the threshold for rational belief. Now as we move through this series of arguments, we get more and more premises and the conclusion becomes a bigger and bigger conjunction. So with each new argument, the conclusion is a little less likely than the one that came before it. At some point, you'll have an argument whose conclusion is right up on the threshold for rational belief. Call that Argument T—T for threshold of course. The next argument in the series will have a conclusion below the threshold for rational belief—call that Argument SubT1. And then, as the series proceeds, you will eventually have an argument whose conclusion is so well below the threshold for rational belief it becomes rational to believe the *negation* of the conclusion. And by the time we arrive back at Exhibit B, the negation of the conclusion is well above the threshold for rational belief—at least according to this guy. Now all the while, as we move through these various arguments, he continues to think each premise is true.

J: Okay but hold on a minute. I was wondering about this before. These are mathematical propositions here. If they are each true, then they each have a probability of 1. 1 times 1 times 1 and so on is still 1. So if you think each premise of Exhibit B is true why isn't the probability of its conclusion just 1?

D: It is standard to assign mathematical truths and other necessary truths a probability of 1. But here some contingent matters are in play. The conjunctions in question are true only if I performed all of those calculations correctly. And since I'm only human, the probability of my performing a certain arithmetic calculation correctly will never be 1. While there may be a sense in which we should say that mathematical truths all have probability 1, we must also recognize our own fallibility. So even though there is a sense in which I might say each mathematical truth on the list has a probability of 1, there is another sense in which I cannot be 100 per cent certain that it is true. This is why I spoke earlier in terms of degrees of confidence. You could also call these attitudes epistemic probabilities.

P: I'd like to know more about what he means by "epistemic probability" here and how we are supposed to calculate it. But I'm willing to let that slide for now. What I'd most like to know is where exactly we cross these thresholds and I'd like to know what we're supposed to think about the various arguments when we do. So I ask the defendant, which of these Exhibits, which argument in other words, is Argument T? Where in the series is the last knowable conclusion?

D: That's a little like asking me how many hairs I can lose before I go bald.

J: How so?

Sorites Paradox

D: Imagine you took someone with a full head of hair and plucked each hair from his head one by one until they were all gone. At the end of this process, he'd be completely bald. But, of course, he was bald before that. George from *Seinfeld* is bald but he has some hair. At what point in the plucking process does someone *become* bald?

J: I see. Baldness is a vague concept. So on one end of the spectrum he's bald, on the other he's not. But there is no exact point in between, no precise number of hairs, where baldness starts. And so I take it you think the various thresholds for rational belief that the prosecution is talking about, those don't exist either.

D: No. Others say that but I think there is a precise cutoff point both for baldness and for rational belief. I just think we cannot know where that cutoff line is. I'm what you call an epistemic theorist about vagueness.[10]

P: Okay. So, if I may continue, Mr. van Kripgenquine believes argument T exists somewhere in my series. In other words, there is a last argument in this series where it is rational for him to accept the conclusion on the basis of the premises. And he also believes somewhere in this series, right after argument T, is argument SubT1, the first argument where the premises are rationally believable but the conclusion is not.

D: That's correct. But like I said, I cannot tell you where those arguments are. I don't know. Neither does anyone else.

P: But they do exist. Somewhere in my series here is argument T and right after that is argument SubT1?

D: That is my position.

P: So if I walked you through the series, asking you whether each of the premises and the conclusion of each argument is true, beginning with Exhibit C and going all the way up and back to Exhibit B, then at some point you'd run across arguments T and SubT1.

D: Correct.

J: Please tell me you're not planning on actually doing that.

P: As long as we agree that we would eventually run across argument T and right after that argument SubT1, we can just discuss it hypothetically. Suppose I've walked the Defendant through each of these arguments and we have arrived at argument T.

D: T's there. But I don't know where. So I won't be able to identify it as the threshold when I do come across it. Neither will you.

P: Understood. But let's just suppose we've started at Exhibit C and worked our way up. You think Exhibit C has true premises and a true conclusion. You think the same about Exhibit D.

---

10 For a defense of this sort of view see Timothy Williamson, *Vagueness* (New York: Routledge, 1994) and Roy Sorensen, *Vagueness and Contradiction* (Oxford: Oxford UP, 2001).

D: Yep. In fact, whenever I believe one of the arguments on the list has a true conclusion I am rationally obliged to say that the next one does too. Otherwise, it would look as if I know where the cutoff is. And I don't.[11]

P: Okay. So if we keep going on up the list at some point we get to argument T. Suppose that's where we are. What would you think about that argument?

D: Since I think the first argument has a true conclusion, I'd be rationally required to think that the second one does too. And the third. If you walk me through the arguments one by one like that I'd have to think that the argument immediately prior to T has a true conclusion too. And so I have to think T does also.

J: Is this supposed to present a problem, Counselor? I thought the idea was that T is at the threshold for rational belief in its conclusion and not below it. Since T's conclusion is true and rationally believable, it ought to be knowable too.

P: The problem happens when we move up from T, the argument with the last knowable conclusion, to SubT1, the argument with the first unknowable conclusion. Suppose I've asked him if he accepts each premise of T and he says yes. And I've asked him if he accepts the conclusion of T and he says yes. Now we move to SubT1. I ask him about each premise and he says of each premise that it is true—this, of course, is what he says for all of these arguments. Now, suppose I ask him about SubT1's conclusion. Would you say that it is true, that it is false, or that you do not know?

D: It wouldn't be rational for me to say that the conclusion of SubT1 is false. SubT1's conclusion is just below the threshold for rational belief but that isn't enough to put its negation at or above the threshold. And I couldn't say that I don't know whether SubT1's conclusion is true either. Since I would have just said that T's conclusion is true and I would have said the same about each of the preceding arguments in the series, if I say that I don't know whether SubT1's conclusion is true then I'd know that I said that and thus it would look like I know where the cut off is. So I'd have to say that SubT1's conclusion is true. And it will be rational for me to do that. Like I said before, if it's rational for me to believe that one argument in the series has a true conclusion, then it is rational for me to believe the next one does too. Since it's rational for me to believe T's conclusion it's also rational for me to believe SubT1's conclusion too.

B: Gotcha!

D: This guy and his gotchas.

---

11 See Sorensen, *Vagueness and Contradiction*, 58.

J: Please explain your gotcha, Bailiff.

B: He just said that it is rational for him to believe SubT1's conclusion. But SubT1 was supposed be the first argument in the series whose conclusion is *below* the threshold for rational belief. SubT1 was defined as an argument whose conclusion is not rationally believable.

P: Exactly, Your Honor. The contradictions are piling up. On his view, it is not rational to believe the conclusion of SubT1 but once you run across it, it is rational to believe the conclusion of SubT1. And notice that this is a straightforward explicit contradiction: it is rational to believe SubT1's conclusion and it isn't. He can't slip out of this one by appeal to these distinctions between believing inconsistently and believing an inconsistency.[12] And the same problem happens in the other direction. If we start with Exhibit B—the argument with the most premises—and work backwards removing premises one by one, the same kind of problem will occur in reverse. He thinks it's rational to believe Exhibit B's conclusion is false. And then he'll be committed to saying the same about the conclusion of the next argument in the reverse series—Exhibit B minus one premise. And you see what will happen from there.

J: But what if, instead of agreeing to walk all the way through your series of arguments there, at some point he just takes the 5th and refuses to say one way or the other whether it's rational to believe the conclusion?[13] He can do that. It's in the constitution.

P: Can someone selectively take the 5th once they've already begun their testimony?

J: I don't know. You're the lawyer. You tell me.

D: Don't forget I haven't even been sworn in fellas.

P: And at what point would you recommend he fall silent? If he stops talking at some particular point, looks like he's still committed to thinking he knows where the cut off is. It might not be the cut off for rational belief. But it would be the cut off for rational assertion. And that should be just as difficult to identify on his view.

J: Then why not just decline to talk about these things at all? Just don't take the stand.

---

12 In *Vagueness and Contradiction*, Sorensen is led from the epistemic view of vagueness to the conclusion that rationality demands we believe infinitely many contradictions.
13 Williamson discusses this strategy in Section 1.2 of *Vagueness*.

P: You do remember he's a philosopher, right? Keeping quiet might be allowed by the country's constitution but it is nowhere in this guy's.

D: Objection!

P: See?

D: Your Honor, I'd like to get it on record that philosophers aren't as bad as everybody thinks. Sure there are a few obnoxious ones out there but these hateful generalizations people make about us arise from a confirmation bias. Humans are constantly guilty of confirmation bias. It's a ubiquitous fallacy of reasoning.

P: Objection. If confirmation bias is ubiquitous, then the evidence for the ubiquity of confirmation bias is nowhere near as good as we think it is. Furthermore, this talk about what he should say as we walk him through these arguments is beside the point. What should he *think* about arguments like Exhibit B? What should any of us think? Even he agrees that since the premises are just simple arithmetic equations that he's checked with his highly reliable calculations, he should think that each premise is true. And since it is just a case of and-introduction, he should think it is valid. But then what should he think about the conclusion? He says we should think it's false. But I can't do that, Your Honor. I can't believe that a valid argument where each of the premises is true has a false conclusion. I don't see how the court can either.

TV Announcer: How would you decide this case if you were in the judge's seat? Would you side with the defendant and say that it is rational to hold inconsistent and perhaps even contradictory beliefs? Or would you decide with the prosecution and say it isn't? Or would you do both? We'll find out what happens when we return right after this important message.

Skepticism Refuted?
A Day in the Life of a BIV

We've all heard this one. There is a brain in a laboratory being kept alive in a vat of bubbly fluid. Its neurons get stimulated by electrodes that are hooked up to a computer maintained by some mad scientists. This brain is being stimulated in exactly the same way your brain is right now. Since perceptual experience is a product of brain stimulation, this brain will have exactly the same experiences you are now having. It thinks it is holding a book. But it is not. It does not even have hands. It is just a brain in a vat.

Now imagine that you are that brain in a vat. How would things look? Wouldn't things look just like they do now? So how do you know *you* are not that brain in a vat? And if you do not know that, how can you know much of anything? How can you know, for example, that you have two hands? This is the problem of skepticism.

Here are some theories philosophers have offered to solve the problem along with some objections and replies. This is intended as a brief overview of some of the arguments. So do not take any of it to be the last word.

Solution 1: Simple Reliabilism. We believe things as the result of various psychological processes. Perception, for example, causes us to believe things about our immediate environments. If a belief forming process produces true beliefs most of the time, then it is *reliable*. Knowledge is true belief formed by a reliable process.[1] Provided the world is more or less the way we think it is, the process of sensory perception will lead us to believe the truth most of the time.

---

1 See Alvin Goldman, "What Is Justified Belief?," in George Pappas (ed.), *Justification and Knowledge* (Boston: Dordrecht Riedel, 1979), 1–25.

For instance, suppose S believes, on the basis of vision, that he has two hands. As long as S is a normal two-handed human being whose visual processes are functioning properly, S's belief that he has two hands will be true and it will have been formed by a reliable process. And thus it will also be an item of knowledge. So, contrary to what the skeptic thinks, we can know things about the world around us.

The "Too Iffy" Objection. This is a merely conditional response to skepticism. The most the reliabilist can say is that we know things *if* our belief forming processes are generally reliable.[2]

Reply. Skeptics are out to prove knowledge is impossible. Reliabilism shows that it is possible. Thus skepticism is refuted.

Solution 2: Neo-Mooreanism. George Berkeley was an idealist who thought the only things that exist are ideas and the minds that perceive them. There are no "external things." G.E. Moore sought to refute idealism with a simple little argument. "Here's a hand," he said. "And here's another. Therefore, there are at least two external things."[3]

The following similar argument provides us with a way to know we are not brains in vats.

> I have hands.
> If I have hands, then I am not a brain in a vat.
> ──────────────────────────────
> Therefore I am not a brain in a vat.

Now you know.

The Circularity Objection. Neo-Mooreans are begging the question. We cannot just come out and assume that the first premise up there is true.

Reply to the Circularity Objection. The fallacy of begging the question occurs when someone assumes his conclusion as a premise. But the conclusion of the above argument does not appear as a premise. Moreover, believing the first premise does not require prior acceptance of the conclusion. Just about everybody believes he has hands; hardly anyone outside a philosophy class has ever heard of brains in vats.

Solution 3: Different Evidence. One can remember that P only if P is true. False memories are like the false bottom on a smuggler's suitcase. That's not really a bottom and that's not really a memory. Likewise, if you see that P, then

---

[2] This sort of point is made by Laurence BonJour in "The Indispensability of Internalism," *Philosophical Topics* 29(1/2): 47–65, 64 (2001) and Barry Stroud in "Understanding Human Knowledge in General," reprinted in *Epistemology: Internalism and Externalism*, Hilary Kornblith (ed.) (New York: Blackwell, 2001), 142.

[3] G.E. Moore, "Proof of an External World," *Proceedings of the British Academy* 25: 273–300 (1939).

P is true. If P is false, then you do not see that P. Seeing that P is a *factive* state. Or, in Gilbert Ryle's terminology, "see" is a *success word*.[4]

A key assumption in the skeptical argument is that brains in vats and normal subjects have exactly the same grounds to believe they have hands. But this assumption is false. The normal subject's grounds for believing he has a hand is his *seeing that he has a hand*. A brain in a vat merely *hallucinates that he has a hand*. These are different things. One of these things entails that the subject has a hand; the other does not. Ergo, brains in vats do not have the same reason to think they have hands as we do. We see that we have hands. They do not and indeed cannot.[5] All they can do is hallucinate that they have hands. Once we acknowledge that, the skeptical argument evaporates. This view nicely complements the Neo-Moorean argument. It shows that I have a reason to accept the first premise of the Neo-Moorean argument that a brain in a vat does not.

The Indistinguishability Objection. The normal subject's experience of seeing that he has a hand and the brain in a vat's experience of hallucinating that he has a hand are *introspectively* and *qualitatively indistinguishable*. From the point of view of the subject, they will appear exactly the same. So how can it be that the normal subject and the brain in a vat have different reasons or that their experiences are completely different kinds of things?

Reply 1. Seeing and hallucinating are qualitatively distinguishable. Dreaming you are being presented to the Pope is "quite obviously not" like being actually presented to the Pope.[6]

Reply 2. Just because seeing and hallucinating *seem* exactly the same does not mean they *are* the same. A lemon shaped bar of soap might look and smell just like a lemon.[7] But that doesn't mean it is one.

Solution 4: Phenomenal Conservatism. In virtue of the kinds of perceptual experiences we have, it seems like we are not brains in vats but beings endowed with bodies and hands. And if it seems to S as if P, then S is thereby *prima facie* justified in believing that P. Unless there is a reason to think we are brains in vats or we lack hands for some other reason (and there is not), we are justified in believing that we have hands because that's how things seem to us.[8]

---

4 The notion of a success word was introduced by Gilbert Ryle, *The Concept of Mind* (London: Hutchinson, 1949), 149.
5 The idea that brains in vats and normal subjects possess different evidence for their perceptual beliefs has been defended in different ways by Timothy Williamson in *Knowledge and Its Limits* (Oxford: Oxford UP, 2002) and by Duncan Pritchard in *Epistemological Disjunctivism* (Oxford: Oxford UP, 2012).
6 J.L. Austin says this in *Sense and Sensibilia* (Oxford: Oxford UP, 1964), 48.
7 Austin, *Sense and Sensibilia*, 50.
8 For an overview see Michael Huemer's "Phenomenal Conservativism" in *The Internet Encyclopedia of Philosophy* (2014). http://www.iep.utm.edu/phen-con/.

The So What Objection. Why does the fact that something *seems* to be true give anyone a reason to think it is true?

Solution 5: Contextualism. Michael Jordon is 6'6". Is he tall? It depends. He is tall for an ordinary person but, for an NBA player, he is not. (Average height of an NBA player in Jordan's heyday was a little over 6'7".) Tallness is contextual. Whether it is correct to say that Jordan is tall depends on the conversational context. Are we talking about Jordan alongside ordinary folks or NBA players? The standards for tallness are of course much higher in the second case.

Something similar is true of knowledge. Whether it is correct to say something of the form *S knows that P* will depend on what is being considered in the conversation. The various alternatives to P that are being discussed is one thing that will set the standard for how good a position one needs to be in to make an utterance of "S knows that P" true.

The skeptic gets us to take the possibility that we are brains in vats seriously and, in so doing, he shifts the conversational context and raises the standards for knowledge. In the context of a philosophical conversation about skepticism, it is true to say "I don't know I have hands" because there the standards for knowledge are extremely high. This explains why skeptical arguments seem so compelling when they are presented. The skeptic has created a conversational context where his skeptical denials of knowledge are true. The way the skeptic talks, you cannot know you have hands unless you can rule out every conceivable way you might be wrong including far out scenarios such as the one where you are a brain in a vat. And once those standards are in place, you cannot win. But no need to fret. In ordinary everyday contexts, the standards are lower. Ordinarily, when I say something like "I know I have hands," what I say comes out true. The skeptic is a little like someone who surreptitiously imposes the NBA standard for tallness (> 6'7") into any conversation about whether someone is tall so that he can "prove" that hardly anyone is tall.[9]

Solution 6: Inference to the Best Explanation. The fact that a hypothesis provides the best explanation for a given set of facts is, in general, a good reason to believe it. For example, suppose you hear scratching in the walls, you notice some cheese has gone missing, and the flour sack has little bite marks in the corner. These facts provide reason to believe the hypothesis that you have a rodent in your house—even though you haven't yet seen a rodent. The hypothesis that you have a rodent in your house provides the best explanation for the facts you have observed.

Now turn to the philosophically interesting example. We have perceptual experiences of various external objects. For example, I am now having a visual

---

9   For a thorough defense of contextualism along with answers to objections see Keith DeRose, *The Case for Contextualism* (Oxford: Oxford UP, 2011).

experience of a pair of hands. Commonsense says my perceptual experiences generally have the features they do because they are caused by and accurately represent various external objects. In this particular case, commonsense says I am having this sort of experience because there is a pair of hands in front of me. The skeptical argument proceeds by offering an alternative explanation for perceptual experience. According to the skeptic, the hypothesis that you are a brain in a vat whose experiences are largely inaccurate and caused by a computer in a laboratory provides just as good an explanation for the various features of your perceptual experience as the commonsense story.

This is where the skeptic is mistaken. For various reasons, the commonsense story is a better explanation for your perceptual experiences than the brain in a vat hypothesis.[10] The brain in a vat hypothesis leaves too many unanswered questions. (Where did the brains come from? How did they get in the vat?) The commonsense story is also much simpler and it fits better with our background beliefs. The commonsense story also explains why we are so often successful in predicting the future courses our experience will take. If perceptual experience is all an illusion, how would we ever know what to expect next? The hypothesis that there is a pair of hands in front of me—and the general commonsense picture of the world that surrounds it—does a much better job explaining why our experiences appear the way they do than the skeptic's hypothesis that we are brains in vats.

The Truth Connection Objection. What makes one proposed explanation for a given set of phenomena better than another? Things like simplicity, congruence with our background beliefs, and predictive success are often advertised as explanatory virtues. But there is no reason to think a proposed explanation that possesses more of these virtues than an alternative is more likely to be true.

In this dialogue, these solutions to the skeptical problem and a few others are explored, defended, and criticized. But there is a twist. The interlocutors are all subjects who believe they are in fact brains in vats. And the familiar responses to skepticism are offered in defense of the claim that the subjects know they do *not* have hands. The main conversation is framed by a discussion among nighttime security guards at some sort of skepticism laboratory.

Larry and Stan are nighttime security guards chatting while bored on the job.

Larry: Okay, I got one. Brain in a vat walks into a bar. Bartender says, "Can I get you a drink?" Brain in a vat says, "No thanks, I already am one."

Stan: Real funny.

---

10 For a detailed discussion and critique of this sort of view see James Beebe, "The Abductivist Reply to Skepticism," *Philosophy and Phenomenological Research* 79(3): 605–36 (2009).

L: You didn't like it? Okay, how 'bout this? Brain in a vat walks into a bar. Some drunk sidles up and says, "Hey, can I smell your hands?" Brain in a vat says, "Absolutely not. I don't even have hands." Drunk says, "Well, then it must be your feet!"

S: Dumb and derivative.

L: Oh, so you want original? You want clever? Brain in a vat runs into a bar, stops abruptly at the counter, and says, "Hey barkeep, gimme a drink." Bartender shakes his head and says, "No way. You're sloshed."

S: Ouch. And how does a brain in a vat run into anywhere? Or walk.

L: Dude. What's your problem? I'm trying to lighten things up around here. I mean, yeah, we're both pulling eight bucks an hour in a crappy night watchman job at some community college science lab making sure somebody doesn't break in and steal a bunch of brains in vats. But that doesn't mean we can't have some fun to pass the time. Geez. Now on that note, any cold ones left in the cooler? I'm dry.

S: Cooler's cashed. But I stashed a sixer on the floor behind the cryogenic freeze chamber. You know, where they keep the zebra? I opened the release valve a little to blow cold air on 'em.

L: Sweet. Why would somebody ice a zebra anyway?

S: No idea. I hope we don't end up thawing the thing out.

L: Meh. We'll just drop it off at the zoo. They'll never know. More important to keep our stuff cold. And well hidden. I'll grab you one too.

S: Don't bother. I'm not in the mood.

L: Listen. I'm getting real sick of your mopey attitude. Either you tell me what's up, or I'm throwing you in there with the zebra.

S: All right here's the thing: You ever wonder what it's like?

L: What what's like?

S: To be a brain in a vat. There you are confined to a tub of 7-Up your whole life just to serve the perverted interests of a bunch of stupid scientists. And then, as a further insult, some know-nothing rent-a-cops make lame jokes and bounce quarters at you all night.

L: Well, it's not like they feel anything. I mean, they're just brains in vats!

S: What are you talking about? Each one of those brains is alive and physiologically the same as a normal one. And they are being stimulated in exactly the same ways. It's just that the stimulation comes from the computer over there by the copier instead of sensory organs. In a normal human being, experiences, beliefs, emotions, and everything else involved in consciousness is just a product of brain stimulation. Doesn't matter the source. Eyes, ears, nose, computer in a lab, doesn't matter.

L: So what are you saying? They have lives just like ours?

S: Seems that way to them. In fact, I overheard one of the whitecoats—you know, the bald one, always has the clipboard?—saying it's rigged up so these brains have the same sorts of perceptual sensations a normal person would. One of those brains over there could be having the same experiences as you right now.

L: You mean dying of thirst while having to listen to your bullshit?[11] Well, I do feel sorry for them then.

S: I'm serious.

L: Well, then wait a minute. If their experiences are the same as ours, it's not like they know they are brains in vats.

S: Exactly. They don't know. But I think they have a right to know. I don't think these scientists can deceive them like that for the sake of some pointless experiment. These are human brains we're talking about here.

L: So what are you going to do? Tell them they're brains in vats?

S: I was thinking about it. You see that microphone on the counter there? Next to the computer? I overheard the shrinks saying it's a brand new brain-in-a-vat voice interface system. You talk into the mic, and the computer processes it and then sends the signal over to the brains, and then they believe what you say. I was thinking I should tell them what's really going on around this place. You know, blow the whistle.

L: So if you talk into the mic, they hear you?

S: Not really. The earliest voice interface systems worked that way. But the problem was they usually wouldn't believe what they were told. Brains can be

---

11 "Bullshit" is now a perfectly respectable philosophical term. The study of bullshit is also a growing sub-branch of philosophical research. For more, see Harry Frankfurt's seminal best-seller *On Bullshit* (Princeton: Princeton UP, 2005).

real stubborn. So the new system bypasses the hearing mechanisms and puts the information right onto the neurons.

L: I don't know, man. They told us not to mess with any of the equipment. Could screw up the experiment. Then what? This job stinks and everything. But after that night with the volleyball team, the college won't let me drive the parking garage shuttle anymore. So I lose this gig, I'm done. Besides, wouldn't that make it worse for them? Wouldn't they get lonely just sitting there knowing they're brains in vats?

S: Lonely? No. They've got it wired up so they can communicate with each other. You see those headphones? That's how the lab techs listen in on what the brains in vats say to each other.

L: Say to each other?

S: Yeah, I know, they don't have tongues. Or ears. But tongue movement is just a product of stuff going on in the brain. They got it rigged so the brain activity that normally causes talking sends a signal from one brain to the other brains. The others receive the signal as the experience of hearing a sound— the same sound that would have been made if the brain was hooked up to a tongue. And you can hear it all with the headphones.

L: But what's their life gonna be like once you liberate them? Aren't they just gonna see a bunch of bubbly fluid and the inside of a glass container? Aren't they worse off that way?

S: I don't know how to control what they see or hear or smell or anything like that. That's done with the computer software, and you need a password to get in. I tried "password" and some dirty stuff, but none of that worked. Scientists are smart.

L: So you're going to tell them that they are all a bunch of brains in vats but their experiences will stay more or less the same? So they'll believe that they see stuff in front of them, but they also believe it's not there?

S: No, here's the thing. You see the chrome box next to the microphone? With the red button on it? That's a reboot switch. I heard the scientists telling one of those tour bus groups the other day about how there was this big problem with the phase 2 voice interface prototypes when they first figured out how to put information right into the brain. The shrinks would speak into the mics, and about half the time, the brains would explode. Huge friggin' mess. And these brains ain't cheap. Turns out some theory says you can't have inconsistent beliefs or something. And then some other theory says a brain has so many beliefs there's no way to know whether a new one will generate a contradiction.[12] That's why they added the red button. You push that, and the brains reboot around what you just said.

L: Reboot?

S: Yeah. The brain believes what you say, and if you reboot, it maintains anything it believed before—provided it preserves consistency. Stuff that's inconsistent with what you said gets tossed. Some new stuff gets filled in so it all hangs together. And it's done seamlessly.

L: Seamlessly.

S: Yeah, in other words, the brain doesn't notice the reboot. It's as if what you told it was something it believed all along. The reboot reboots the brain's memory too, I guess.

L: Whoa.

S: Yeah. The system's brand new. It's an external device they haven't installed into the computer. So you don't need the password to use it. But it won't be like that for long. If I'm gonna do the right thing, I need to move quick.

L: Whatever. Long as I got nothing to do with it.

S: Yeah, okay. Why don't you go grab us a couple of those zebrews?

L: Way ahead of you.

After Larry leaves, Stan pushes the red button and speaks into the microphone. "Your perceptual experiences are illusions generated by a computer controlled by mad scientists. There are several of you, and you can communicate with each other through wiring the scientists have installed. But you are, all of you, just brains in vats." He then puts on the headphones.

Subject 948: Your body illusion is looking good, Subject 237. Have the mad scientists who control all of our consciousness been regularly subjecting your brain to workout experience simulations?

Subject 237: Indeed. My pleasant hallucinations of eating and drinking were becoming closely correlated with very unpleasant body illusions. Luckily there's a new program running. Thanks for noticing, 948. What have you been merely appearing to do for fun lately?

---

12 See Christopher Cherniak, *Minimal Rationality* (Cambridge, MA: MIT P, 1986).

948: I've been enjoying a computer-generated sequence of illusory fishing experiences.

237: Followed by fish illusions?

948: No. But I guess that's why we call them fishing hallucinations and not *fish* hallucinations!

237: Tell me something I don't know.

Subject 43: Hey brains, what up?

948: Oh hey, Subject 43. I was just talking about 237's body illusion and how tight it merely appears to be lately. I mean just take a second yourself and enjoy those bicep-shaped sense-data he's got going on.

43: That's interesting because I've been thinking a lot about our various hallucinations of physical objects lately.

237: Oh yeah.

43: Yeah. Lemme ask you guys this: What if we actually have bodies? Instead of everything we've ever thought about the universe, what if all of our experiences are not illusory but veridical? What if—contrary to what we all think—experience accurately represents real things in an external world? What if, instead of this being an illusion of a hand, it's a real hand?

948: How is that even possible?

43: Well, imagine all your experiences are caused by sensory organs responding to external objects in a brain-independent spatiotemporal world. I don't mean the mere illusions of sense organs that we receive from the computer when we merely appear to look into a mirror. But real eyes, ears, and noses. In other words, what if we're not brains in vats but *brains in skulls*, which are inside bodies, and our sensory experiences are accurate, and we just think we are brains in vats who hallucinate all the time?

237: Oh boy. Here we go, Mr. Philosopher!

948: Yeah, really. Brains in skulls? C'mon! Everybody knows we're in vats. It's common sense!

43: But think about it. We believe there's a computer causing us to have illusory experiences, but how would it look if our experiences were veridical? It would look just like this! So how can we know we don't have hands? We all believe that. But how can we know? How do you know you're not just a brain in a skull?

237: Like he said, common sense.

43: It's important to preserve common sense only if we start from the assumption that common sense is mainly correct. But that's exactly what I'm challenging. I'm asking for some sort of evidence for these commonsense beliefs we have.

237: Okay, I'll play. Let's grant there's a "possible world" where brains like us inhabit skulls instead of vats. And in that alternate reality, those poor saps are totally wrong.

948: Hang on. Shouldn't the brains in skulls think they are looking at hands?

43: Maybe you could have a case like that. But I'm imagining a situation where a brain in a skull has all the same experiences, reasoning processes, and beliefs that you do. If you like, you can imagine an exact duplicate of yourself inside a skull, which is inside a body, which inhabits a world where all this stuff we hallucinate is real. And that stuff gets accurately represented to the brain through sense organs instead of through a computer in a mad scientist's lab. Now, since that brain is identical to you, it too will believe that the world it experiences is an illusion, that it doesn't have hands, and all the rest. So my question is, how do you know you're not that brain in a skull?

237: Yeah, yeah, I get it. They think they don't have hands and that their experiences are mere hallucinations just like we do. But they're totally wrong. I'll grant you that's a possibility. The mistake happens when—

948: Wait. Should we really grant that's a real possibility? How did the brains get in the skulls in the first place? And if there are no mad scientists to provide nourishment, who keeps them alive? Do they have comwires? If not, how do they talk to each other? You're gonna have to spell out some details here before you can get me to buy the idea that brains in skulls are possible. Otherwise you're just leaving too many unanswered questions.[13]

43: Okay. Well, what if, instead of a scientist putting it there, the brain is somehow born into a skull and then—

237: I've got a much cleaner way to handle this if you brains would let me appear to talk. Look, knowledge is simply true belief formed by a reliable process.[14] My belief that I do not have hands was formed by the process of counterperception—a process we employ all the time, every day. I am confronted

Simple Reliabilism

---

13 Compare William Lycan, *Judgment and Justification* (Cambridge: Cambridge UP, 1988), 189–90.
14 Compare Alvin Goldman, "What Is Justified Belief?," in *Justification and Knowledge*, George Pappas (ed.) (Boston: Dordrecht Riedel, 1979).

with a perceptual image such as this hand-shaped sense datum. And this causes me to believe that I do not have a hand. Given the relevant sensory inputs, the same sort of process generates all sorts of true beliefs about what the world isn't like. This foot illusion, for example, generates the belief that I do not have a foot. Given that I am a brain in a vat who is constantly being fed hallucinations by a team of mad scientists, the familiar process of counterperception will produce true beliefs most of the time.

43: But then what about the brain in a skull who forms that same belief by the same process but ends up always wrong?

237: His counterperceptual belief-forming processes are totally unreliable. But that's his problem. As long as our counterperceptual processes are reliable, we know we don't have hands.

43: But how do you know counterperception is reliable?

237: Don't confuse knowing with knowing that you know. To know that P I need to form a true belief that P via a reliable process, but I do not need to know that the process is reliable. You say knowledge is impossible. So all I need to do is lay out the conditions under which it is possible for me to know that I do not have hands. And I did. It is possible that my belief that I do not have hands is true and produced by a reliable process.

> Is there reason to think the normal reliabilist response to skepticism offered in the introduction is better than this flipped version? One can ask this kind of question throughout this dialogue.

948: You know, I thought 43 was out of his vat there at first, but now I'm thinking he might be on to something. I want a reason to think I know that I do not have hands. You've given me a reason to think it's possible that I know. But I want a reason to think knowledge is actual. I don't think you can give me that unless you can show that 43's brain in a skull hypothesis is actually false, not just possibly false.

> Neo-Mooreanism

237: Oh, that's all you want? A reason to think I'm not a brain in a skull looking at real hands? Well that's easy. This is a hallucination of a hand. So is this. Therefore, I'm not a brain in a skull looking at real hands.[15] QED, BIV.

43: You're begging the question.

237: Not at all. The fallacy of begging the question, that is, "circular reasoning," occurs when a subject's belief in a premise of an argument is epistemically dependent on prior acceptance of the conclusion of that argument.

43: Uh huh. And that's exactly what you just did.

237: No, I didn't. Look at it this way. I hadn't even thought about the possibility that this might be a real hand because I am a brain in a skull until you

---

15 Compare Moore, "Proof of an External World," 273–300.

showed up and started going on about it. Ergo, my belief that this is a brain in a vat's hallucination of a hand is certainly not grounded in a prior acceptance of the proposition that I am not a brain in a skull. So there's no fallacy of circular reasoning going on here.

948: Well, I'm glad you brought that up because this has been bothering me all along. From the fact that these are hand hallucinations, why does it follow that I don't have a hand? Couldn't a brain with hands still hallucinate hands?

237: How's that?

948: Well, in 43's science fiction story it's the eyes rather than a computer that regulates the brain in a skull's visual sensations. But what if something gets messed up along the way? Suppose the eyes are closed, but somehow the brain still produces a hand image. This would mean that the brain in a skull hallucinates a hand and, at the same time, has hands. From the fact that this is a hallucination of a hand it doesn't logically follow that I don't have hands.

237: Two things. First, the argument was this: These are hallucinations of hands; therefore, I am not a brain in a skull looking at real hands. That follows. Second, your understanding of "hallucination" is confused. Maybe you can introduce a sense of "hallucinating that P" where it is compatible with P's being true. And if you are unfortunate enough to be a brain in a skull, I guess what you described might happen. But that's not how we use the phrase. Under our common everyday conception of it, hallucinating is antifactive. In other words, hallucinating that P entails not-P; "hallucinates that" is an antifactive mental state operator or AFMSO.[16] That's just how we use the term in our language.

43: It is?

237: Yeah, it is. Somebody looks up and says he's hallucinating a hawk circling above him. And then you convince him there really is a hawk where he's looking with exactly the features he's experiencing. Well, he'd surely retract his claim that he was hallucinating it. "Hallucinate" is a failure word.[17] But if you want to insist that you can hallucinate that P when P is true, then just take my use of the words "hallucination," "illusion," "image," and the like to mean *mere* hallucination, *mere* illusion, and *mere* image. If S merely hallucinates that P, then not-P. And since I'm merely hallucinating that I have hands, it follows that I don't.[18]

---

16 Compare Williamson, *Knowledge and Its Limits*, 34.
17 Compare Gilbert Ryle, *The Concept of Mind* (London: Hutchinson, 1949), 149–53.
18 Compare Duncan Pritchard on the factivity and reflective accessibility of "seeing that P" in *Epistemological Disjunctivism*.

43: But that's the whole point! The brain in a skull will say the same thing. But he's got a hand! So how do you know it's a mere hallucination rather than a veridical experience?

237: If it appears to walk like a mere duck-shaped sense-datum, appears to quack like a mere duck-shaped sense-datum, then, well, you know the rest.

948: I want to be on your side, 237, but I think you're ignoring 43's point.

237: No I'm not. Just attend to the features of your experience. Isn't this exactly what a computer-generated hallucination of a hand would be like? It has visual aspects that appear three dimensional, it generates olfactory sensations. You can even superimpose your tongue-shaped sense-datum over it and generate taste sensations.

948: That's kinda gross.

237: Not for me. What data have your hand illusions been overlapping lately? 43 demands we produce evidence that this is a hand illusion rather than a real, brain-independent hand. What more evidence could you possibly want than the very features of that experience? Anyone who pays attention to those features and applies our normal epistemic procedures will get the result that this is a hallucination of a hand.

948: He's raising a challenge to our normal epistemic procedures.

237: But if the only acceptable response is to step outside my vat and directly compare my brain's hallucinations against objective reality, then the "challenge" is nonsensical. This passes every conceivable test we have for being a computer-generated hand image. To continue to suggest it might be something else makes no sense.[19]

948: I want to agree with you, but that still doesn't seem like an adequate response.

237: You should note something else very peculiar about 43's "challenge." He's demanding that we somehow disprove his hypothesis that these are real hands because we really are brains in skulls. But he's given us no reason for thinking his far-out science fiction hypothesis is true. He's not provided any reason to think we are brains in skulls. He is just—in true philosopher's fashion—floating it as a possibility. He hasn't rationally motivated the idea that I am a brain in a skull, he's merely raised it.[20] Now maybe if he were to provide some sort of

---

19 Compare O.K. Bouwsma's "Descartes' Evil Genius," *Philosophical Review* 58: 141–51 (1949).
20 Compare Pritchard's, *Epistemological Disjunctivism*, 124.

positive support for his strange hypothesis, a simple appeal to experience and our ordinary everyday epistemic procedures wouldn't do. But as of right now, I don't see why I owe 43's screwball idea any more attention.

948: But he's trying to defend a skeptical position here—we don't know one way or the other. You can't expect him to give evidence that you are a brain in a skull.

237: Exactly. Not only has he not given us reason to think we are brains in skulls, on pain of contradiction, he can't give us that. But, as I've already noted, our perceptual experience provides tons of evidence for thinking we are hallucinating. So, in the absence of any defeaters, we are justified in believing that we do not have hands.

948: I agree this thing looks just like a brain in a vat's hand image. Sure. But doesn't it also look just like a hand? So, isn't our evidence just as good either way?

43: That's what I've been saying all along. If we were brains in skulls, our basis for thinking that we don't have hands would be exactly the same.

237: There's another place where we disagree. Suppose you have two cases. In one case, the one commonsense tells us is real, we are brains in vats whose perceptual experiences are all hallucinations generated by a computer that is controlled by a bunch of mad scientists. Call that the Good Case. In the other case, we merely think we are brains in vats whose experiences are illusory but really we are brains in skulls accurately representing a brain-independent external reality. Call that the Bad Case.[21]

43: Okay. Good Case: brain in a vat, hallucinating mere images of hands; Bad Case: brain in a skull, experiencing real ones.

948: Sounds right. Got it.

237: Now, 43's argument presupposes that the evidence in these two cases is the same. I disagree. The subject in the Bad Case has different evidence.

Different Evidence

948: But the two are indistinguishable. So the evidence is the same.

237: Just because two things look the same doesn't mean they are the same.[22] Skeptics can't just stipulate that the evidence is the same in both cases.[23] Furthermore, in the Good Case, your evidence for thinking that you do not

---

21 Compare Timothy Williamson, "Scepticism and Evidence," *Philosophy and Phenomenological Research* 60: 613–28 (2000).
22 Compare Austin, *Sense and Sensibilia*, 50.
23 Williamson, "Scepticism and Evidence," 616.

have a hand is that you are hallucinating a hand. Ex hypothesi, the poor saps in the Bad Case are not hallucinating. They actually see hands. Ergo, they don't have the same evidence we do. This is the cure for the skeptical disease.

43: I feel a relapse coming. Even if seeing and hallucinating are different things and thus different types of evidence, the question of whether you know you don't have hands then just becomes a question of whether you know you are hallucinating rather than seeing. And how do you know that?

237: Again, don't confuse knowing with knowing that you know. Also, like I said before, hallucinating that P is both antifactive and reflectively accessible. In other words, I can know via introspection that I am hallucinating that P.[24] Now before you say "But a brain in a skull will also think he is hallucinating and he's wrong," don't take what I said to mean that I can discriminate my hallucinations from their corresponding veridical perceptions. I can't. But unless there is a defeater—and there isn't—knowledge doesn't require discriminating evidence; it only requires favoring evidence.[25] So yes, if I were in the Bad Case, I'd think I was hallucinating, and I'd be wrong. But since I know I'm hallucinating, I know I'm not in the Bad Case.

948: I think I've identified what bothers me about your response to 43's skeptical challenge. Let's go back for a second to something I mentioned earlier. Let's imagine a case, kind of like the Bad Case, but where the subject correctly believes he is a brain in a skull. In other words, suppose you had a subject who believes his experiences accurately represented a real hand-filled world, and suppose that in fact they do. And he bases this belief on his veridical experiences of hands. Call this the Not So Bad Case. Seems like you should say that the subject in the Not So Bad Case knows that he has hands. He sees rather than hallucinates his hands; he believes that he has hands, and his belief is based on the fact that he sees his hands.

237: Uh, okay. So what?

948: You think the Good Case and the Bad Case look the same from the inside, right?

237: They look the same from the inside, but evidentially speaking they are not the same. In the Good Case, the subject is hallucinating; in the Bad Case, he isn't.

---

24 Compare Pritchard, *Epistemological Disjunctivism*, 13.
25 Pritchard, *Epistemological Disjunctivism*, 77–100.

948: Okay, so, aside from the fact that his beliefs differ, things will look the same in Not So Bad Case too. The Not So Bad Case will be one where the experiences are indistinguishable from the other two.

237: That's correct. And I suppose, if we set aside what they believe, the evidence in the Not So Bad Case and in the Bad Case will not just look the same but it will be the same—since they both see rather than hallucinate hands. But don't forget a subject in the Good Case will have different evidence.

948: I get it. Now here's my problem. Given my current experiences, how do I decide what to believe? If I start with the assumption that I am a brain in a vat, I can say I am in the Good Case because I hallucinate hands. But if I begin with the assumption that I am a brain in a skull, I can just as easily say I am in the Not So Bad Case because I see hands. Why believe one over the other?

237: This Not So Bad Case is another philosopher's invention. And we certainly have no reason to think it actually obtains. What kind of nut would believe he actually has hands? Even 43 is not that crazy. It's much more natural to think that we're all in the Good Case, and thus we are hallucinating hands. All you need to do there is appeal to the experience itself and follow our normal epistemic procedures.

948: I could imagine someone who thinks he is in the Not So Bad Case saying it's natural to believe you have and see hands. I think what's going on here is that the arguments you are offering in response to 43's challenge aren't really what's doing the work. You are beginning with certain commonsense assumptions about the way the world is—the very assumptions 43 is challenging—and then you are building a philosophical theory on top of that. But this means all your philosophical theories never really address the challenge.

237: Lemme make it real simple. 43 says I am not justified in believing that I do not have hands. But it sure seems like we are brains in vats hallucinating hands. Even 43 agrees with that, right? Now, if it seems to S as if P, then S thereby has at least a prima facie justification to believe that P.[26] And it seems to me that this is a computer-generated hand image. Therefore, I am justified in believing that's what this is. And therefore skepticism is false.

Phenomenal Conservatism

43: So if something seems true, it is?

237: No. Pay attention. If it seems to S as if P, then S has a *prima facie* justification to believe that P; the fact that it seems like this is a brain in a vat's hand hallucination will justify me in believing that's what it is if there is no defeater.

---

26 Compare Lycan, *Judgment and Justification*, 168.

And again, you've presented no reason to think I am in fact a brain in skull. So, the way it seems stands.

948: But why does it seem that way? And why does it seeming that way justify you in believing anything?

237: The answer to your second question lies in the answer to the first. The basis of my perceptual seeming is the content of my perceptual experience. It seems to me that this is a brain in a vat's image of a hand in virtue of the content of my current perceptual experience. My perceptual experience is telling me *that this is a brain in a vat's image of a hand*. This content is asserted by my experience.[27] So, naturally, that's how things seem to me. Now, to answer your second question, a visual experience with the content that P can provide a noninferential basis for belief that P. So my belief that this is a brain in a vat's image of a hand is noninferentially justified by my current perceptual experience.[28]

948: Suppose we accept the theory that a perceptual experience with the content that P can immediately justify a belief with that same content. Why should we also accept your claim about the content of your experience? Why should we think your experience has the content you say it does?

237: You think I might be wrong about the propositional content of my own experience?

948: You introduced this claim about the content of your experience as an answer to a challenge to your commonsense picture of the world. But I'm worried that you've got things upside down. Do I believe I don't have hands because my experience tells me so, or do I think my experience tells me so because I believe I don't have hands?

237: I don't know what you mean, 948.

43: I do. You claim your present sensory experience has the content that this is a brain in a vat's hand image. But this is not an intrinsic feature of experience. You think your experience has this propositional content only because you are already indoctrinated into your commonsense ontology. Someone who did not already accept our commonsense account of the world would never claim that his experience has the content you say yours does. Someone who took himself to be in the Not So Bad Case, for example, would say his experience has the content that this is a real hand. And someone with no prior assumptions about

---

27 Compare Chris Tucker, "Why Open-Minded People Should Endorse Dogmatism," *Philosophical Perspectives* 24: 529–45 (2010).
28 Compare James Pryor, "The Skeptic and the Dogmatist," *Noûs* 34: 517–49 (2000).

the nature of reality wouldn't be able to say anything one way or the other about the propositional content of his perceptual experience. His experience would be one great blooming buzzing confusion.[29] Your claim about the content of your experience is a product of your commonsense worldview. And thus it cannot be used to undermine a skeptical attack on that worldview.

948: The situation would be helped, 237, if you could come up with an independent argument to show that the content of your present experience is what you say it is.

237: The propositional content of an experience is present to the mind simply by virtue of having the experience, independently of any beliefs about what external states of affairs the experience is connected with. That is the model of experience I employ.[30] And, as I said, this experience quite obviously has the content that this is a brain in a vat's image of a hand.

43: That's an argument?

237: The content of a visual experience is, roughly, the content of the belief that it tends to produce.[31] Experiences like this tend to produce in me the belief that this is a brain in a vat's hand image. Therefore, that's its content. And that's an argument.

948: But once again, couldn't someone who accepted the brain in a skull ontology just as easily say her experiences typically cau—

Subject 707: What up brains? I'm so glad your illusions are appearing before my consciousness. I need some info. Any of you brains know if the mad scientists will be running the bank illusion tomorrow? I gotta deposit some bitcoin by Monday to cover my rent. I tell ya, a crystal vat's nice, but, oh man, is it pricey!

948: Hey, 707. We're kinda in the middle of a conversation here.

707: What's it about?

237: Oh, you'll love this. 43's been wasting our time trying to convince us that, in spite of everything we've ever believed all of our lives, we might just be brains in skulls whose experiences reflect objective reality and as a result nobody knows anything. Can you believe this guy?

> Is there another argument 237 might offer to demonstrate his perceptual experience has the content he says it does that does not presuppose that his own "commonsense" picture of reality is correct? Is there a corresponding argument us (allegedly) normal humans could make for thinking our experiences have the contents we like to think they do? Does it matter if no such argument can be found?

---

29 This nice phrase comes from William James's *The Principles of Psychology* (Cambridge, MA: Harvard UP, 1981 [1890]), 462.
30 This line is taken directly from Pryor's paper "The Skeptic and the Dogmatist," 519.
31 This is taken directly from David Lewis's paper "Veridical Hallucination and Prosthetic Vision," *Australasian Journal of Philosophy* 58: 239–49, 239 (1980).

707: Nothing you can do to win that one.

948: Another skeptic?

707: Nope. I just said there's no way to win that argument.

948: And why's that?

Contextualism   **707:** Here's what happens when somebody like 43 shows up. What he does is he introduces some far-out possibility—such as the possibility that we are really just brains in skulls—and, in doing so, he shifts the conversational context. You see, in our ordinary conversations, we claim to know lots of things but far-out possibilities like the one 43 is kicking around just aren't in play. For example, suppose the mad scientists are running an extended hallucination of a walk in the garden.

948: Is it one of the smooth and predictable group hallucinations like the scientists normally generate in us? The kind we both remember afterwards? Or is it one of those chaotic disorderly and scarily unpredictable individual programs the scientists feed us every 18 hours or so?

707: Let's suppose it's a group one. Like the one we're having now.

43: I've wondered about that distinction too. Here I am thinking I'm being fed a group hallucination same as you guys. But how do I know this isn't one of those solipsistic hallucinations?

237: The solipsistic ones are unpredictable. But we can all predict you'll keep making those same stupid arguments.

707: Anyway, suppose we're enjoying an extended group hallucination of a walk in the garden, and I say "Hey, look, there's a goldfinch illusion nestled inside that bush-shaped sense-datum." Now you might ask, "How do you know it's not a woodpecker illusion?" And in response I might point to specific features of the illusion—color, shape, size, you know, stuff like that—that indicate that it's a goldfinch illusion rather than a woodpecker illusion. And, given my expertise in bird hallucination identification, I can rule out the possibility that it's a woodpecker illusion.[32] So, in that context, I can truthfully say, "I know that's a goldfinch hallucination." If asked to defend that, I'd point out those characteristic features, my answer would be accepted, and that would be the end of it.

948: But then why did you say 43 always wins the argument?

---

32   Compare J.L. Austin, "Other Minds," in *Philosophical Papers*, 3rd edition, J.O. Urmson and G.J. Warnock (eds.) (Oxford: Oxford UP, 1979), 50.

707: In ordinary contexts, I know it's a goldfinch illusion because I can rule out the possibilities that are in play in that sort of conversational situation. For example, that it's a woodpecker illusion, a squirrel illusion, and so on. But then 43 introduces some far-out possibility, such as the possibility that I am a brain in a skull, and thus it isn't an illusion of any kind but a real goldfinch. And this is a possibility I cannot rule out. Because, as he keeps repeating, a real goldfinch will look just like one of your garden-variety goldfinch hallucinations.

43: Exactly, so you never know anything.

707: Not so fast. You see, normally these wacky possibilities are not on the table. So, ordinarily, it is true to say "I know that's a goldfinch illusion" because, in ordinary conversational contexts, I don't need evidence that excludes far-out possibilities such as this distant possible world where I am a brain in a skull who sees a real goldfinch. All I need is evidence good enough to rule out woodpecker illusions and the like. But once you bring in this far-out sci-fi stuff—brain in skulls and whatnot—you create an extraordinary philosophical context where it is no longer true to say "I know that's a goldfinch illusion" because the meaning of that utterance has shifted. By getting us to take these goofy possibilities seriously, 43 creates a situation where the standards of knowledge are so high, you cannot truthfully assert a knowledge claim any more. But, no need to fret; this is not the normal sense of "knowledge." Ordinarily, the standards are much lower. In one sense, he wins; in another sense, everyday knowledge remains untouched. So don't let this guy bother you. If you say "I know I don't have hands," you say something that is true most of the time.[33]

948: I'm having the same feeling I did right before you showed up, 707. You are beginning with the assumption that our commonsense story of being brains in vats is correct. And this allows you to call the kind of story that 43 proposes—where we are brains in skulls—a "far-out" possibility. So the theory isn't really doing anything. The real meat of it is the framework of commonsense beliefs you are starting from—the philosophy is just so much word gravy. Your "solution" in essence begs the question.

707: In saying that my ordinary claims to know are true, I betray my conviction that I am a brain in a vat and that I do not have hands. These are things 43 thinks I do not know. Indeed, I am ready to admit to 43 that if I am a brain in a skull, then under any standards for knowledge I do not know that I do not have hands. But, of course, as I firmly believe, I am not a brain in a

---

33 Compare Keith DeRose, "Solving the Skeptical Problem," *Philosophical Review* 104: 1–52 (1995).

skull. Is it legitimate for me to use this conviction in a debate against 43? Not if we're playing King of the Mountain Illusion. But if 43 is marshaling deeply felt intuitions of mine in an attempt to give me good reasons for accepting his skepticism, it is legitimate to point out that other of my beliefs militate against him and ask why I should give credence to just those that favor him.[34]

237: I just noticed another thing rotten with 43's position.

43: What's that?

237: This suggestion that the bulk of our commonsense beliefs might be false, the whole idea that 43's brains in skulls would be massively mistaken, betrays a failure to understand elementary semantics.

948: Please explain.

237: It's crucial to 43's argument that the brain in a skull has all the same beliefs you do. This is why 43 thinks the brain in a skull is wrong when he has an experience like this and says "This is a hand hallucination." But this assumes that the contents of our thoughts are completely determined by internal factors. In other words, since your enskulled counterpart's brain is a molecular duplicate of your brain, he believes exactly what you believe when his brain is in the same state as your brain. But this is all confused because the contents of our thoughts are at least partially determined by external factors, that is, by the kinds of things that typically cause them.

43: I don't know that I agree with that. But even if it's true, so what?

237: So the brain in a skull's veridical experiences are caused by real hands, real trees, and the like. Our hallucinatory experiences are caused by computer circuits and other stuff controlled by mad scientists. And it is from their experiences that both types of brains learn to think and talk. So brains in skulls cannot refer to or even think about hand hallucinations—at least not in the way we do. When the brain in a skull says "This is a computer-generated hand hallucination," she does not have the same thought you have when your brain uses those words. You learned to say, "This is a computer-generated hand hallucination" in the presence of a computer-generated hand hallucination. Thus, in your language "computer-generated hand hallucination" refers to a computer-generated hand hallucination. But in the brain in a skull, what typically causes the thought, "This is a computer-generated hand hallucination" is a real hand.

43: Exactly! That's why the brain in a skull is wrong.

---

34 This is taken almost verbatim from DeRose's "Solving the Skeptical Problem," 50.

237: No. That's what I've been trying to tell you. You are assuming those words have the same content for us brains in vats as they do for those brains in skulls. But in Skull English, terms like "hand hallucination" and the brain states associated with those terms do not refer to hands-in-the-image as they do for us. Given the brain in a skull's environment and given the way it learned its home language, thoughts involving terms like "hand hallucination" will refer to their typical causal sources, namely, hands-in-the-flesh. And that is how the brain in a skull's utterances get their propositional content. So when a brain in a skull says, "This is a hand hallucination" in the presence of a real hand, what he says is true. And the same holds for utterances like "This is a tree hallucination," "This is a fish hallucination," and so on. These too will have different contents in Skull English—contents that allow that the brain in a skull will be mostly correct in her commonsense beliefs.[35] So the so-called Bad Case is not one that involves massive error. And once we realize that, your whole argument falls apart.

707: Well, as y'all know, I'm fully in favor of semantic solutions to epistemological problems but this one ain't gonna do it.

237: And why's that?

707: All 43 needs to do to block this move is introduce the case of the recently enskulled. Instead of imagining a brain identical to ours but who has always been inside a skull, imagine a brain that lived its whole life normally just like us in a vat. But this one was taken out of the vat and enskulled five minutes ago. And imagine it was done seamlessly so that the brain didn't notice it. That brain would be thinking in Vatglish but living in Skulltown. And so when it says "This is a hand hallucination" in the presence of a real hand, it really is wrong. Your semantic theory might handle the skeptical hypothesis of the always enskulled, but it won't handle the recently enskulled.[36]

237: Well, that's real clever, but it doesn't matter. I still say it is incoherent to think we could be massively mistaken in the way 43 thinks we might be. And there's an even simpler way to prove it.

43: Oh, yeah?

237: Yeah. Suppose there is a being who is almost omniscient. He knows every fact there is to know about the world including all of the facts about my brain activity. The only thing this being does not know are the contents of my thoughts; he does not know how to assign meanings to my various neural

---

35 Compare Hilary Putnam, *Reason, Truth and History* (Cambridge: Cambridge UP, 1981), Chapter 1.
36 Compare Anthony Brueckner, "Brains in a Vat," *Journal of Philosophy* 83: 148–67 (1986).

firings and simulations of speech. Then one day this being sets out to do just that. The omniscient interpreter, like all interpreters, will have to employ the principle of charity. He will have to interpret my thought and speech simulations in such a way that they largely agree with his own point of view. And since he is omniscient, his point of view is also objectively correct. So the omniscient interpreter will ascribe beliefs to me in such a way that most of them are true. Therefore, most of my beliefs are true. And the same argument goes through for my enskulled counterpart. There could be an omniscient interpreter who employs the principle of charity to interpret the brain in a skull's linguistic behavior. And since the interpreter is omniscient, he will ascribe mostly true beliefs to the brain in a skull. Therefore, most of the brain in a skull's beliefs are true. And therefore, even if I am a brain in a skull, most of my beliefs are true. The argument generalizes to any subject, actual or possible. Massive error about the world is simply unintelligible.[37] Belief is in its nature veridical.[38]

948: That's a good one. But like I said before, if we start from the assumption that we are brains in skulls who do have hands, we could just as easily appeal to the omniscient interpret—

237: I'm really getting sick of this. Lemme make it even simpler. The best 43 has is a deductive argument with the conclusion that we don't know that we don't have hands. But it is obvious that we do know that we don't have hands. This is far more obvious than any philosophical premise 43 might appeal to in support of his position. So 43 hasn't provided any reason to doubt that we don't have hands. The most he's done is given us a reason to doubt whatever philosophical premises he used to reach his ridiculously implausible conclusion.[39]

707: Hey, look, there's 1781's illusion going by. Just like clockwork. Whatcha up to 1781?

Subject 1781: As you can hallucinate, the mad scientists are imposing my regular walk illusion upon our faculties.

43: You know, I wonder a lot about these mad scientists too. What's their world like? What are they like? Do they live in vats too? Or are they immaterial spirits? Is their knowledge unlimited? Are they omnipotent? Do they love us? Do they have free will? Do they live forever?

---

37 This line is taken from Donald Davidson's essay, "The Method of Truth in Metaphysics," *Midwest Studies in Philosophy* 2: 244–54, 245 (1977).
38 See Davidson's essay, "A Coherence Theory of Truth and Knowledge," in *Kant Oder Hegel?*, Dieter Henrich (ed.) (Stuttgart: Klett-Cotta, 1983).
39 Compare Lycan's argument in "Moore against the New Skeptics," *Philosophical Studies* 103: 35–53 (2001).

237: Borrrr-RING!

1781: Your questions are not answerable, 43. To attempt an answer would be to engage in transcendental employment of the understanding to the unconditioned laboratoumenal reality that lies beyond all possible experience. The principles of understanding are a priori principles of the possibility of experience and all a priori synthetic propositions relate only to experience and wouldn't be possible otherwise.[40]

237: Is it just me or does this guy never make any sense?

707: Well here comes 1933. I'm sure he'll set us straight.

43: Hi '33. Looks like the run time on your solitude in the mountain hut program has ended. Can you believe none of these guys can prove we aren't just brains in skulls who are completely mistaken about the world? That's quite a scandal if you ask me.

1933: I, the *Vatsein*, in apprehending illusions, am always already in a vat. Being-in-the-vat itself belongs to the determination of my own Being. The question of whether these are illusions at all and whether their Emptiness can be proved, makes no sense if it is raised by *Vatsein* as Being-in-the-vat; and who else would raise it? The "scandal of philosophy" is not that this proof has yet to be given, but that *such proofs are expected and attempted again and again*.[41]

707: Clears it right up.

237: Looks like the party's just starting. Here comes Subject 6.0001275.

43: Hey there, 6 point. I've been meaning to tell you there was a police illusion looking for you the other day. Something about a child brain that got squashed in, maybe with fire poker illusion? Anyway, what's your take on skepticism? Do I know I don't have hands?

Subject 6.0001275: If I were to ask myself "Do you lack hands?" I should not make sure by checking the illusions the computer sends me. For why shouldn't I test *the computer* by checking to find out whether it is sending me illusions of hands? *What* is to be tested by *what*? The questions that I raise and my doubts depend on the fact that some propositions are exempt from doubt, are as it were like the vat that holds the brain in place. That is to say it belongs to the logic of my scientific investigations that certain things are *in deed* not doubted. I just can't investigate everything. If we want the brain to turn, the vat must

---

40 Compare Immanuel Kant's *Critique of Pure Reason*, Paul Guyer and Allen W. Wood (trans.) (Cambridge: Cambridge UP, 1998 [1781]).
41 Compare Martin Heidegger, *Being and Time*, John Macquarrie and Edward Robinson (trans.) (Oxford: Basil Blackwell, 1962), Section 43.

stay put. My life consists in being content to accept many things. Now I would like to regard this certainty, not as something akin to hastiness or superficiality, but as *a form of life*.[42]

707: Oh boy.

Inference to the Best Explanation

948: You know gang, I think it's becoming clear to me that the only hope for solving 43's puzzle lies in recognizing that the commonsense story we all believe is a much better explanation for why we have the perceptual experiences we do than this brain in a skull business. Like I said way back when all of this started, the commonsense story leaves fewer unanswered questions. Also, on the commonsense story, our experiences all stem from a single cause: the mad scientists' computer. That's much simpler than the brain in a skull hypothesis which requires our perceptual experiences to be caused by a nearly infinite number of *different* things. And simplicity is, as they say, the seal of truth. Now another virtue of the commonsense story is that it fits with our background beliefs about the world whereas this brain in a skull hypothesis conflicts with almost everything we know. Not to mention the fact that 43 has postulated these mysterious real objects in a totally *ad hoc* manner. And of course the commonsense story makes our experience much more predictable. Based on my past experience, I have lots of information about the kinds of illusions the mad scientists send me so I can predict that future illusions will tend to behave in more or less the same way. But if my experiences are all caused by a bunch of ontologically independent real objects, how can I have any idea what they'll do next? Put all that together and you get plenty of reason to think the commonsense hypothesis is much more reasonable because it's a much better explanation than the brain in a skull story.

43: But there's no good way to measure simplicity. And, even if there is, why think the simpler theory is more likely to be true? And your point about fitting with background knowledge is just another appeal to commonsense—which is the very thing I'm challenging. The point about unanswered questions amounts to the same thing. And why should we assume our questions about the world are answerable anyway?

948: Well think of it this way. The skeptical position says that the brain in a skull hypothesis—or BIS as I'll call it—explains my perceptual experiences just as well as the commonsense hypothesis that we are brains in vats. Here's a reductio ad absurdum on that idea. Earlier this morning, when I was enjoying a fishing illusion program, I had a certain set of visual experiences E. Based on E, I adopted the belief that the computer was sending me an illusion of a

---

42 Compare Ludwig Wittgenstein, *On Certainty*, Denis Paul and G.E.M. Anscombe (trans.) (New York: Harper and Row, 1969), Sections 125, 341–44.

smallmouth bass. Call that belief SB. But then I reflected upon E a bit more carefully and noticed that this sense datum was one where the mouth image extended back beyond the eye shape. So naturally I arrived at the belief that the computer was not sending me an illusion of a smallmouth bass but of a largemouth bass. Call that belief LB. LB is a better explanation for E than SB. Now, at the end of the day, the skeptic has to say that BIS, which in this case would entail that I was faced with a real largemouth bass, is just as good an explanation for E as LB. But if BIS is just as good as LB and LB is better than SB then it follows that BIS is a better explanation for E than SB. In other words, that I was faced with a real largemouth bass is a better explanation for my experience than the commonsense hypothesis I originally believed. But a skeptic certainly cannot think that any skeptical hypotheses are ever a *better* explanation for experience than a commonsense one. The skeptical position is that it's always a tie. But as the example shows, that is not sustainable.[43]

43: I never said it's always a tie. There might be some hypotheses that involve commitment to the commonsense ontology that are so bad they do a worse job explaining experience than a skeptical hypothesis. That doesn't mean you should believe either one. And the real issue, like I said before, is why the fact that a certain hypothesis exhibits various explanatory virtues better than its competitors—if it is a fact—gives us a good reason to believe it. No one has defined these explanatory virtues in any precise way and, even if they have, no one's demonstrated a connection between exhibiting explanatory virtues and being tru—

Stan's eavesdropping is suddenly interrupted when he feels an intensely cold sensation on his neck. He looks up to see Larry laughing and holding a 16-ounce can against his skin. Stan removes his headphones.

L: Gotcha! Woo! These things are cold. Good idea, stashing 'em behind the cryogenic freeze chamber.

S: Larry, what took you so long? And who's the guy in the mesh t-shirt?

L: Smoke break. This is Rico. You don't know him? Dude rocks. He was running the floor buffer out in the hallway, and I asked if he wanted to help us soak up some suds.

Rico: Stan the man. Good to meet you, dude. Cool earmuffs. What's the scuttlebutt over there in Seavattle, Illusionois? Any of those little guys seen *The Matrix* yet?

---

43 Compare Jonathan Vogel's argument in "Internalist Responses to Skepticism," in John Greco (ed.) *The Oxford Handbook of Skepticism* (Oxford: Oxford UP, 2011), 544.

S: Seattle's in Washington.

R: Huh?

S: Interesting you should bring up *The Matrix*. Larry, do you remember how I said one of those brains could, at least from his own point of view, be exactly the same as you right now?

L: Did you find one like that? Awesome! Always wanted a son.

S: You're sitting here making fun of these brains in vats but how do you know you're not one of them? How do you know you're not just a brain in a vat?

L: You think I'm a brain in a vat? Well, watch me bust open this tallboy. Boom! There you go. I refute it thusly. BIV don't crack no PBR. That must be the worst part of it. Am I right, fellas?

S: But a brain in a vat could have an experience indistinguishable from your own experience of popping that Peeber. So how do you know you're not in the vat?

R: Oh, look at you, Stanley! You wanna throw down some epistemology? And here I was thinking you security guys just came in here and took naps on a pile of mail. Well, I'm game, my friend. It is on.

L: Yeah, Stan. Rico here's a certified philosophizer from NYU. Just like Patrick Swayze in *Road House*.

S: Any particular discipline?

R: Not really. Man's search for knowledge. That kinda crap.

S: Find any answers?

R: Loads of 'em. Bachelors are unmarried. Water is wet. Pain is identical to C-fibers.

S: C-fibers don't hurt.

R: I don't normally talk about this philosophy stuff to ordinary people—Epictetus advises against it, you know.[44] But you guys seem alright, and I wouldn't want you to go getting all depressed over some skeptical pseudo-problem. So let me clear the dust here.

S: Hit me.

R: Here's the thing, provided our perceptual processes are reliable, any true beliefs produced by them will constitute knowledge. Now, I know some people

---

[44] Epictetus, *The Enchiridion* Nicholas P. White (trans.) (Indianapolis: Hackett, 1983), fr. 46.

whine about how reliabilism doesn't properly take evidence into account. Blah, blah, blah. Doesn't matter. Go ahead and bring evidence in all you want because, after all, the evidence a brain in a vat has is totally different. We see hands; they hallucinate them. What better evidence could you want than what your experience tells you? And experience is telling us that this right here is a hand. Now, if you still want to sit there and insist that I need to disprove some far-out brain in a vat story in order to know anything, all you're really doing is introducing some extraordinary sense of "knowledge" with these super-high standards where it becomes impossible to know anything in that sense. But in any ordinary everyday context, we don't worry about distant possible worlds like that. So our knowledge ascriptions will still be true most of the time. Furthermore, anybody who thinks we could be massively mistaken is woefully ignorant about some of the most important developments in semantics of the last few decades. But we're gonna need more than a sixer if you guys want me to break all that down for you.

S: Some of what you said there sounds familiar. But imagine I am fully convinced that I am in fact a brain in a vat. Instead of thinking that this is a hand, suppose it seems totally normal for me to think it is a mere image of a hand generated by a computer controlled by a bunch of dorks in long white coats. And then suppose that some "skeptic" comes along and suggests that maybe I'm not a brain in a vat. Maybe I'm a brain in a skull, and this a real hand! Couldn't I use everything you just said to support the claim that I know I don't have hands? For example, couldn't I say, brains in skulls see hands and I'm hallucinating them? Or if I found it natural to think I am a brain in a vat, wouldn't I say that the content of my current experience is that this is a mere image of a hand? And isn't that a problem? I mean doesn't that show that these theories of yours aren't really doing anything? Aren't you just assuming your commonsense worldview at the outset—which is the very thing in question—and then sticking some epistemological theory on top of it? Or to put it another way, what am I supposed to believe? Am I supposed to believe I am a brain in a skull and I have hands, or am I supposed to believe I am a brain in a vat and I don't? Whichever one I choose, I can endorse any of those philosophical theories to justify it. Doesn't that mean the theories are just some empty foam on top of an ultimately unquestioned commonsense ontology?

R: Whoa! Flipping my arguments on me? That's some jiu-jitsu mind stuff there, Stannyboy. Brains in skulls! I never heard that one before. But the move does remind me a little of Law's paper on the argument from evil[45] and

---

45 In "The Evil God Challenge," *Religious Studies* 46: 353–73 (2010), Stephen Law considers the possibility that the world was created by an omniscient, omnipotent, and perfectly evil creator. The problem for this view is that it seems obvious that goodness exists in (continued)

of Steen's parody of psychological egoism.[46] And Borges's short story "Tlön, Uqbar, Orbis Tertius" does something similar with Berkeley's idealism, of course.[47] But being just a night watchman, you wouldn't know anything about that stuff. Anyways, look, this little trick of yours doesn't raise any problem for these solutions to skepticism. The most it would show is that if I am a brain in vat, I can know I don't have hands. But since I'm neither a brain in a vat nor a skeptic, that doesn't bother me. In fact, this is exactly what any non-skeptic should expect: brains in vats can know they don't have hands just as we know we do have hands. Sounds good to me. And now that I think about it, I'm not so sure all these responses to skepticism can be flipped so easily. Take contextualism, for instance. That's a theory about the semantics of "knows" in our language. But brains in vats aren't part of our linguistic community. No telling what goes on over there. So maybe one of these theories works one way and not the other for some reason. Now if it does, that'd mean that theory is superior to the others in an important way. So I gotta admit: vatterizing solutions to skepticism is a novel way to think about these issues, and it does seem to present a new way to test them. It also seems to show that the classic skeptical paradoxes really leave us with two problems. First, the obvious: Do we know anything? But even if we answer that, there's a separate ontological problem: are we brains in vats or brains in skulls? An answer to the first I guess won't always answer the second. And hey, what you said about the theories "not really doing anything" makes me wonder whether this a new way to think about what it is to beg the question. This move might even be some sort of operational test for whether a theory is guilty. You know, it's too bad you're not a real philosopher like me because you could write this thing up and publish—

Your eavesdropping is suddenly interrupted when you feel an intensely cold sensation on your neck. You look up to see your workmate laughing and holding a cold can against your skin. You may now remove your headphones.

---

the world. Why would such a being allow that? The usual responses to the argument from evil can be flipped and applied here with the same degree of success they usually enjoy—or so it would seem. John Collins pursues the idea further in "The Evil God Challenge: Extended and Defended," *Religious Studies* (forthcoming).

46 In "Why Everyone Acts Altruistically All the Time: What Parodying Psychological Egoism Can Teach Us," *Philosophia* 39: 563–70 (2011), Mark Steen considers the hypothesis of psychological altruism—the idea that all human action is motivated by selflessness. The argumentative moves typically made by the psychological egoist are inverted and applied in defense of this opposing psychological theory.

47 See Jorge Luis Borges, *Labyrinths* (New York: New Directions, 1962).

Pragmatic Encroachment
Hanna and Rosana Case the Bank

According to some, whether S knows that P depends at least in part on how important it is that S is right about P. The higher the stakes are for you, the harder it is for you to know. In *Knowledge and Practical Interests*, Jason Stanley offers the following pair of cases to support this view.

Low Stakes

Hannah and her wife Sarah are driving home on a Friday afternoon. They plan to stop at the bank on the way home to deposit their paychecks. It is not important that they do so, as they have no impending bills. But as they drive past the bank, they notice that the lines inside are very long, as they often are on Friday afternoons. Realizing that it isn't very important that their paychecks are deposited right away, Hannah says, "I know the bank will be open tomorrow, since I was there just two weeks ago on Saturday morning. So we can deposit our paychecks tomorrow morning."

High Stakes

Hannah and her wife Sarah are driving home on a Friday afternoon. They plan to stop at the bank on the way home to deposit their paychecks. Since they have an impending bill coming due, and very little in their account, it is very important that they deposit their paychecks by Saturday. Hannah notes that she was at the bank two weeks before on a Saturday morning, and it was open. But, as Sarah points out, banks do change their hours. Hannah says, "I guess you're right. I don't know that the bank will be open tomorrow."[1]

Many think what Hannah says in each of these cases is true. She knows the bank will be open in Low Stakes and she does not know this in High Stakes. But the only relevant difference between the two cases is that in Low Stakes, it does not matter whether the bank will be open tomorrow, while in High Stakes, it does. So, the argument goes, it must be that whether S knows that P depends at least in part upon how important it is that S is right about P. This is known as the "pragmatic encroachment" thesis.

The following dialogue is a variation on Stanley's bank cases where one interlocutor is a proponent of the pragmatic encroachment thesis.[2] In this story, the stakes oscillate throughout the course of the conversation. And the reason for stopping by the bank is a bit different from what it is in Stanley's examples. You will also notice that Hannah has evidently gotten rid of Sarah and one of the letters of her name.

Hanna and her wife are sitting in their parked Chevrolet El Camino in front of First National Bank while the stereo plays.

Hanna: Hot out here. And your music only makes it worse. Do you have to constantly play this awful band?

Rosana: It's about to get hotter in there. And what do you mean awful? You hear that voice? The bass? That guitar? Those drums? The lyrics? What other power trio has a range like this? They've got a hard rock phase, a Hobbit rock phase, an Ayn Rand phase, a smooth jazz phase and—my personal favorite—this synth-heavy electronic phase from the early 80's. Not as popular with the fans as their other stuff but a significant conceptual development if you ask me.

H: I guess everything is just a phase.

R: I used to think that in my youth.

---

1   Jason Stanley, *Knowledge and Practical Interests* (Oxford: Oxford UP, 2005), 4.
2   Stanley's bank cases are themselves a variation on cases offered by Keith DeRose in "Contextualism and Knowledge Attributions," *Philosophy and Phenomenological Research* 52(4): 913–29 (1992).

H: This might be a bad idea today.

R: Yeah?

H: Yeah. Look at that line. The place is crammed. No telling what can happen when you have that many people milling around. We didn't take this kind of crowd into account on our dry run.

R: No problem. We walk in there, wave the artillery, get everybody on the ground, grab the dough and go. Just like we planned.

H: Just like we planned? You see this traffic? Don't even think about making a left outta here. It'll take at least 160 seconds over what we planned just to turn right. And that concrete barrier in the median? That wasn't there the other day. Forget about a quick U-turn. We've gotta refigure our whole route. And that's *if* we don't get popped inside or out here in the parking lot. Who robs a bank on a Friday afternoon? Worst possible time.

R: What are you saying?

H: Let's hit the joint tomorrow morning. Less traffic. Fewer eyeballs. Still plenty of cash.

R: Do you know if it's open tomorrow? Lots of banks aren't open on Saturday.

H: Yeah, I know this one's open.

R: How do you know that?

H: I was just here a couple of weeks ago. Remember? When we took our savings out to open a checking account at Second National?

R: Do *I* remember? How about do *you* remember I spent my whole morning today scraping char off the sourdough. What kinda bank is desperate enough to give away toasters to new customers? And what kinda toaster do you think you're gonna end up with?

H: Not my fault you threw away the owner's manual.

R: I wouldn't have had to if you'd've cleaned out that kitchen drawer like I asked.

H: When've you ever *asked* me to do anything?

R: Look, if we're not gonna get the money today, it's really important that you're right about this place being open tomorrow. The Gooch is expecting us to pay him on Sunday. We don't do that, we got big trouble.

H: I don't wanna have to go underground.

R: The Gooch'll put you there if he doesn't get his money by Sunday. You were here a couple weeks ago but banks change their hours sometimes. So we don't know whether the place is open tomorrow. We gotta hit it now.

H: Why don't I just go up there and check the hours?

R: Yeah. Go up there with no mask on, all those cameras and all those people around, check the hours and then, if they're not open tomorrow, come get me and then we'll go right back up and rob the place. Great idea.

H: I don't need to check anyway. I know it's open. I was just here a couple Saturdays ago.

R: Not good enough.

H: Why not? I mean, how did we know Denny's would be open this morning? Because we were there a couple weeks ago. Same thing.

R: Denny's is always open. And yeah, ordinarily, a reason like that might suffice for knowing that the bank will be open tomorrow. But when you are trying to figure out whether someone really knows something, you can't just focus on the reasons. You've also gotta consider the stakes.

H: The stakes?

R: With The Gooch involved, the stakes are high. Way too high to know based on a reason like that. It's a classic case of pragmatic encroachment.

H: Pragmatic encroachment? Please tell me that's not more of Professor Peart's prattle.

R: It's the idea that in addition to the traditionally recognized epistemic factors—belief, truth, evidence—all knowledge is determined by practical interests. In general, the more important it is that an agent is right about whether P, the better a position she needs to be in to count as knowing that P. And in this case it's very important that you are right in your belief that the place will be open tomorrow—it's literally life and death. So you don't know. But you might if it mattered less.

H: So you're saying that being here a couple weeks ago is not enough for me to know that the bank will be open tomorrow. But, in less serious circumstances, I could know it on that very same—

R: Is that him?

H: Who?

R: Over there, coming right this way!

H: Crap.

Hanna and Rosana stash their weapons beneath their seats as a small, thin man in a shiny dark suit approaches the vehicle and taps the car window with his pinky ring. Rosana rolls the window down and plays calm.

R: Hey there, Mr. G. Nice threads.

The Gooch: Afternoon, ladies. Nice ride.

H: It's a '69.

G: I know. And look how clean she is. I'd sure hate to see anything happen to her.

H: Don't worry, Mr. G, we'll have the money like we promised.

Ring

G: That's mine. [*gets out phone*] Yeah.... Uh-huh.... Done. [*puts away phone*] What were you saying?

H: I said don't worry, we'll have it by Sunday.

G: Don't worry? Do I look worried, Hanna? Am I sweating? What if I was worried? Am I supposed to stop worrying because you told me to? Are you giving me emotional advice now? Are you my therapist? Like I need to come lay down on your couch? I got some kinda problem with my mother or something? What do you know about my mother?

H: Uh, I didn't mean to—

R: Dammit, Hanna.

Long awkward pause

G: Oh man! If you could see the looks on you two's faces right now. In my business, we call that Pesci-ing somebody. I wish the guys coulda seen it. Classic! Anyways, look. I got good news. Seems I'm going out of town on business for a few days. That's what the call was about. Good thing I'm already at the bank. I gotta grab some bread to spread.

R: You keep your money in the bank?

G: Mattresses get robbed. And banks keep records. But a certain Panamanian casino don't. Which makes it a good place to make some dirty money disappear when it needs to. But what am I telling you two for? The point is I'm not gonna need the money from you 'till week after next.

R: Well thanks, Mr. G.

G: You caught me in a good mood. But don't tell nobody. It'll ruin my image. You two ladies have a nice weekend. I gotta go in for some green. Can you believe there's a line out the door? I thought these places just kept money. Looks like they're giving it away! Good thing people around here know who I am. Made guys don't wait in no lines.

The Gooch heads toward the bank.

R: God. What a twit.

H: But didn't you hear what he said? We've got until the week after next to get the money! That's enough time for the check from my dad to clear. So we don't need to rob the bank!

R: Yeah that's great.

H: It sure is.

R: Alright. Let's get out of here.

H: You know, I just remembered. When I moved the money over to Second National, I left a few bucks here. Nowhere near what we owe The Gooch of course, but enough for us to get a couple pitchers and a nacho plate this weekend. While we're here, maybe I should go in and pull that out—legally of course—and then we can have a little celebration tomorrow night.

R: I'm not waiting in those lines. And I'm sick of sitting in this hot car.

H: But what about the nachos?

R: We'll just drop by here tomorrow and get some cash when the lines are shorter and the traffic's not so bad. We know it'll be open.

H: We know it'll be open?

R: Yeah. You were just here two weeks ago.

H: What?

R: I said you were just here two weeks ago.

H: I know what you said. But you also said that wasn't good enough.

R: That was when it mattered more. Now nothing turns on it. Just some nachos. Didn't we go over this already? Geez, it's like you never listen to me, Hanna.

H: What?

R: Exactly.

H: I get the idea that whether we know the bank will be open depends on how important it is. But how do you go from thinking we didn't know the bank will be open tomorrow to thinking we do know it now even though I never got out and checked the hours?

R: Easy. When The Gooch needed the money by Sunday, it was really important for you to be correct in thinking that the bank would be open tomorrow. Those high stakes made it hard for you to know. But once The Gooch decided he didn't need the money until the week after next, it didn't really matter whether you were correct in thinking the bank would be open. So we went from not knowing it to knowing it. You never got out and checked the sign but so what? Like I said, knowledge isn't just a matter of evidence. It's also a matter of the stakes.

H: Wait a minute. Before The Gooch walked up, you were ready to go in there and rob that bank at the worst possible time all because we didn't know whether it'd be open tomorrow. But now you say we do know that. But it's not like the bank changed its hours while we were talking. The whole time we've been out here, it's always been the case that the bank will be open tomorrow. Even when we were planning on going in there and robbing it today!

R: That's right. But before The Gooch changed his mind, it was still really important whether the bank is open tomorrow, so important we didn't know. Yes, we could've turned around and come back tomorrow. And if we had, we'd've found it open. But we didn't know that at the time. Given how important it was, we couldn't have known that.

H: But that's what we should've done. Turned around and come back tomorrow. That would've been rational. Right?

R: Wrong. It wouldn't have been rational for us to turn around and leave on the assumption that the bank would be open tomorrow because we didn't know that then. But we do now. So let's go.

H: Well I'm just glad The Gooch is off us for awhile. That guy makes me nervous.

R: The Gooch. Do we even know if he's a real mobster? I'm starting to think he's full of crap. What's he talking about making money disappear? What is that?

H: I think it has something to do with laundering.

R: Well I think I saw it on *Mike Hammer*. And did you hear him say, "don't tell nobody cause it'll ruin my image"? Dude drives a Camry. And speaking of laundry, what's with that suit? I'm pretty sure I saw that thing on the rack at Zayre's last Thursday. I bet if we never paid him, nothing would happen.

H: Looks like he's headed back over. Maybe you should ask him about the suit.

The Gooch approaches the El Camino.

R: I see you're back from the bank, Gooch. Did the nice teller give you a lollipop?

G: What? Can't hear you over your radio ladies. Reason I came over, my plane don't leave for another four hours. And there's this money I need to get rid of. So I thought the three of us maybe we could—

Ring

G: That's me again. [*puts phone to ear*] Got it. No problem, they're right here. Done. [*puts phone away*] I'm glad you're still hanging around ladies. There's been a change of plans. Looks like my little vacation's canceled. Which means I will need the money by Sunday after all. You understand. You understand *completely*. I'll see you two at the usual spot day after tomorrow.

R: No problem, Mr. G, sir. Have a nice day!

The Gooch walks away and Rosana removes her pump action Mossberg from under the driver's seat and chambers a round.

R: Alright. Let's do this!

H: What?

R: You heard him. He needs the money by Sunday. That check from your old man won't clear 'till later in the week. That leaves us with one option. Lock and load baby! Well I guess that's two.

H: Slow down, Rosana. Now he wants the money by Sunday. I get it. But I thought we agreed it'd be better if we came back and hit the bank tomorrow.

R: We can't just come back tomorrow because we don't know whether the bank will even be open tomorrow. Didn't we go over this already?

H: Couple times. But just a few seconds ago you said we know the bank will be open tomorrow. Remember? So why don't we come back and do it then?

R: I remember. But don't you remember it didn't matter then? And now it does.

H: I got that. But look: Knowledge is factive, right? In other words, S knows that P only if P is true.

R: Yeah. So what?

H: So after The Gooch left the first time and it didn't matter, you said, "We know the bank will be open tomorrow." S knows P only if P. So what you said entails that the bank will be open tomorrow. If it weren't true that the bank will be open tomorrow, we couldn't have known it would a few minutes ago. So let's come back and do the thing then when it's safer.

R: You are assuming when I said "We know the bank will be open tomorrow," I said something true.

H: Well didn't you?

R: I don't know.

H: You don't know.

R: Yeah. I don't know. I certainly believed at the time I said it that we knew that bank will be open tomorrow. But now I don't know whether what I said was true. You see, in those circumstances, we had all the evidence we needed to be in a position to know that the bank will be open tomorrow given that nothing but nachos turned on it.

H: Yeah. So we knew then that the bank will be open tomorrow. And if we knew it a few minutes ago, then it's true. Therefore the bank will be open tomorrow. So let's bail.

R: Not so fast. I mean we met all the requirements for knowing that proposition in that situation *right up to the truth requirement*. Like you said, S knows that P only if P is true.

H: So you're saying we *didn't* meet the truth requirement? So now it's *false* that the bank will be open tomorrow?

R: I'm not saying that. I'm saying right now we don't know whether it's true or false that the bank will be open tomorrow. But *if* it's true that the bank will be open tomorrow, then I was correct to say "we know that the bank will be open tomorrow" back when it didn't matter. But now The Gooch needs his money by Sunday. So it matters big time—like I said, it's life and death. That means right now we don't know whether it's open tomorrow. And if we don't know whether it's open tomorrow, we don't know whether we knew it earlier.[3]

H: So we might've known earlier that the bank will be open tomorrow. But now that it matters so much, we definitely don't know that. And since we don't know that now, we don't know whether we knew it then. But maybe we did.

R: Now you're talking.

H: But wait a minute. You also said you think The Gooch's not even really connected. So how's it life and death?

R: When I said The Gooch is a phony, it didn't matter whether he was or not because he didn't need the money right away. So, that's another one where, provided it's true, I knew it. But you see, now if we operate on the assumption that he's a poser and blow the guy off, there's a decent chance our heads'll end up the same way.

H: Blown off.

R: Exactly. So we can't know now that he's not a real gangster, even if we knew it then. The stakes are too high.

H: And the Camry?

R: Makes a good cover if he is the real deal. *Consumer Reports* says it's a very reliable automobile. And he did seem to get in and out of the bank pretty quick. Still can't explain that suit though.

H: Hold on. Go back to the question of whether the bank is open tomorrow. The idea was that we can't know that the bank will be open tomorrow because the stakes are too high. But that assumes that being wrong about it will get us killed. But now you're saying we don't even know whether The Gooch is legit mob or not. So maybe nothing turns on it. So you don't know whether the stakes are high or not. And if you don't know that, you can't say we don't know the bank will be open tomorrow. Maybe The Gooch is a poser and the stakes

---

3 Hanna's challenge here is often called "the factivity problem." It has been raised as a problem for pragmatic encroachment theories of knowledge and contextualist theories. For a statement of this problem as applied to contextualism, see my "Contextualism and Semantic Ascent," *The Southern Journal of Philosophy* 42(2): 261–72 (2004). Rosana's answer to the challenge is essentially the same as the one offered by Anthony Brueckner and Christopher Buford in "Contextualism, SSI and the Factivity Problem," *Analysis* 69(3): 431–38 (2009).

are low and so we *do* know it'll be open. Or at least we would know it if we believed it.

R: You can go ahead and believe he's a phony but you still wouldn't know it. Because believing he's a fake and acting on that belief might just get you killed. So that's another case where the stakes are too high to know.

H: Still seems like when you say "we don't know whether the bank will be open tomorrow" you're presupposing that the stakes are really high which is to presuppose The Gooch is the real thing, which is something you now say you don't know. In other words, you can't say we don't know the bank will be open unless you know The Gooch is what he says he is.

R: No it's enough that there's a realistic chance that he's connected. And, despite the Camry, there is. That's enough to make the issue of whether we'll get killed if we don't pay him by Sunday a *serious practical question*.[4] And that's enough to make the stakes high. Speaking of Camrys, Gooch's still sitting over there sitting in his. Wonder what he's doing.

H: Let me ask you this. What if The Gooch comes back one more time and says he doesn't need the money by Sunday? So the stakes drop back down. What will you say then? Will we then be able to know the bank will be open tomorrow?

R: I don't know.

H: You don't know?

R: Of course not. This is no different from asking whether I was correct to say "We know the bank will be open tomorrow" earlier back when it didn't matter. Given the situation, we had all we needed to know the bank will be open tomorrow *provided it is true that the bank will be open tomorrow*. Imagining a hypothetical case in the future where the stakes drop back down is no different. If we move back to a low stakes context, we'll have all we need to know that the bank will be open tomorrow provided the bank will be open tomorrow. Right now that's the most I can—Oh, I see you're screwing on your silencer. Good. I knew you'd come around to reason Hanna. You always do. Do you think I should go with this ski mask or my rubber Nixon head? I'm thinking the crowd will appreciate Tricky Dick a little more but I'm worried about the exaggerated nose making it hard for me to see. I like a good visual pun as much as anybody but it seems a little impractical. What do you think?

---

4   For discussion of what constitutes a serious practical question see Stanley, *Knowledge and Practical Interests*, 92–97.

H: I'm not going into the bank Rosana.

R: Then how are we going to pay The Gooch? And why are you fooling around with your piece?

H: It's a philosophical experiment. Me and my gun are going to refute your theory.

R: I don't know what you're talking about, Hanna. But before you go doing anything rash I'll have you know that some recent and very exciting results in experimental philosophy and cognitive science have been found to be highly favorable to the sort of view I hold. With continued funding, I think researchers will find the same empirical results duplicated in—Hey, where are you going?

Hanna stuffs the silenced pistol into her waistband as she exits the El Camino. She walks across the parking lot and approaches the driver's side of a white 2006 Toyota Camry and raps on the window. As the driver lowers it, Hanna removes the pistol and raises it to the driver's forehead. Rosana hears a muffled Ka-THUD. Hanna casually walks back to the El Camino and sits inside.

R: Holy crap. What did you do?

H: Do we know whether the bank will be open tomorrow?

R: What?

H: Do we know whether the bank will be open tomorrow?

R: What the hell are you talking about?

H: I just drilled a tunnel through the middle of The Gooch's head. He won't be needing the money anymore. Now that nothing turns on it, do we know whether the bank will be open tomorrow?

R: Jesus.

H: DO WE KNOW WHETHER THE BANK WILL BE OPEN TOMORROW? Last time I ask.

R: Okay, okay. Sure. We know the bank will be open tomorrow because you were just here two weeks ago. But before you go accusing me of contradicting myself, don't forget that before you got out of the car and murdered somebody, the stakes were much higher so we were in a different epistemic situation. We know now the bank will be open tomorrow but we didn't know it then because too much turned on it.

H: Got it. Now let me ask you this. Suppose for some reason the stakes go back up—as high as they were before. What then?

R: Unless you've got a brain donor and a roll of duct tape, I don't see that happening. But whatever. If we go back to a high stakes situation, we won't know that the bank will be open tomorrow because the stakes will be too high. Now what was your little stunt supposed to prove?

H: If the stakes go back up, we won't know the bank will be open tomorrow. But it'll still be true. Correct?

R: Sure. If The Gooch magically wakes up and the stakes are arisen with him, the bank's not going to change its hours. But, I remind you, we will not *know* that the bank will be open tomorrow.

H: What about the issue of whether he's a real mobster or not?

R: It's pretty clear he's a fraud. So you just shot a guy who was no threat at all, probably just some middle school teacher from the county. I doubt his widow will get much for the Camry now that it's a crime scene. But that's on you. I still want to know why this is supposed to present a philosophical problem for me.

H: Right now we know that the bank will be open tomorrow. Suppose a miracle occurs and The Gooch comes back from the dead and wants the money by Sunday. I bet you'll say we have to rob the bank now because we don't know whether the bank will be open tomorrow—just like you did before. You'll also take back your claim that he's not a real gangster. Just like before, you'll say too much turns on it. Maybe we knew it before when it didn't matter but we don't know it now. So we gotta rob the bank. Right?

R: Gee, before he starts busting our chops about the money, I reckon The Gooch'd want to address the issue of you spilling brains all over his fine Japanese velour. And of course there's the matter of how the hell I'm supposed to know what I'd say or think if I lived in a world where zombie gangster wannabes drive around in blood soaked Camrys to do collections. And don't they kill zombies by taking off their heads? So if your head's already blown off can you even become a zombie? Sounds pretty far-fetched. But I can tell you're upset so I'll let that slide and say yeah. Okay. If the stakes go way up again and we desperately need the money, I'll say we don't know whether it's open tomorrow so we should hit the bank now. And I'll be right. Again.

H: But it's still true that the bank will be open tomorrow. In other words, if the stakes go back up, that has no effect on what hours the bank keeps?

R: I suppose not.

H: So, in that case, it would be better if we left and came back tomorrow.

R: No. You are forgetting that what is rational for a person to do in a given situation is a function of what she knows in that situation. If the stakes go back up and we take off, we are acting on the assumption that the bank will be open tomorrow. But, in that situation, we won't know whether it is true that the bank will be open tomorrow. And it is appropriate to act on a proposition only if you know it is true.[5] So if the stakes go back up, it won't be rational for us to leave and plan on doing the bank tomorrow morning.

H: Maybe it won't be "rational" in the strictest philosophical sense for us to leave in that situation. But wouldn't we still be better off if we did? We'd have a better chance of pulling the job off without getting arrested or killed.

R: Suppose we're at the track. And suppose, just as a matter of fact, Snow Dog is gonna win the next race. Not because it's rigged or anything. Suppose that's just what's going to happen. You could say that there is a sense in which we'd be "better off" if we put everything we have on Snow Dog. If we did, we'd win. Trouble is, we don't know that. If we find ourselves at the track, it's not rational for us to bet a huge pile of cash on a pony unless we know she's the winner. Likewise, if we are in a situation where the proposition that the bank will be open tomorrow is true, there might be a sense in which we'd be "better off" if we left and hit it tomorrow. But since we don't know that proposition is true, we can't say it will be rational for us to act in that way.

H: There's a difference between the horse race and the bank thing. Take a different kind of horse race. Suppose it is rigged. Suppose you are the one who rigged it. And suppose you are real good at rigging races. So you know Snow Dog's going to take the purse.

R: Okay then go ahead and lay your money down. But note that even if you've rigged it, you can't be absolutely certain your efforts will succeed. So there's still a way the stakes could get high enough to prevent you from knowing. But I'll set that difficulty aside. You know on solid grounds that Snow Dog's gonna win. The grounds are solid enough to license a big bet. Go ahead. What's the point?

H: Suppose there's something preventing you from getting to the ticket window to place your bet in time.

---

5   Rosana is here stating what is known as the knowledge norm for action. For more on this idea, see John Hawthorne and Jason Stanley, "Knowledge and Action," *Journal of Philosophy* 105: 571–90 (2008).

R: Like what?

H: I don't know. A guy's mopping the floor in front of the window and he's in your way. And the floor's real slippery. And there's only a few seconds to post.

R: If I were a skilled race rigger, I think I'd plan the betting part out a little better. But anyway, yeah, get a running start, lower your shoulder, slide right through him and get to the window.

H: Okay. Since you know Snow Dog's gonna win, it's rational for you to place the bet and resolve to remove any obstacles that might prevent you from doing that.

R: Sure.

H: Now suppose that there's no janitor in the way but somebody just snuck a pill into your drink. In a few minutes, the pill will cause you to forget you've rigged the race. And you know that once you forget that, you won't be inclined to place the bet.

R: Then get up there and make the bet now.

H: The window's not open yet. And there's a line. And you know that the pill will already take effect by the time you get to the head of it. Once you get up there, you won't be inclined to make the bet anymore. Should you find some way to get yourself to make the bet even though you won't be inclined to do it?

R: How do you recommend I do that?

H: I don't know. Write the bet down and put it an envelope to hand it to the clerk when you get to the window. Or get somebody else to make the bet for you. The point is, since you know Snow Dog's gonna win you should do anything you can to keep your future self from missing out on the opportunity to place the bet.

R: Fine. I don't know if the envelope thing will work though because once you get up there you might just walk off. But I see your point.

H: Okay. Now suppose the pill you've been slipped isn't guaranteed to make you forget Snow Dog will win but it has a good chance of doing so in the next few minutes. Does that make any difference as to what you ought to do? Since you know Snow Dog will win, shouldn't you still do whatever you can to prevent your future self from bumbling and missing the bet?

R: I don't see why not.

H: Wonderful. Now let's think about the bank again. We know now that the bank will be open tomorrow. So we know that if we have to rob it, we have a better chance of success if we do it tomorrow. We also know that a future self of ours might end up not knowing this proposition. But not because of anything directly or even indirectly connected to its truth. A future self of ours might end up not knowing that the bank will be open tomorrow just because of an increase in the stakes. If that happens, we might end up robbing the place today which is a very bad idea. Whether or not The Gooch wants the money by Sunday has nothing to do with what hours the bank keeps. Just like whether or not somebody slipped a memory pill in your drink has nothing to do with whether or not Snow Dog will win. So, by the same argument, shouldn't we do anything we can to prevent our potential future epistemic selves from robbing the bank today?

R: Such as?

H: Let's resolve that, no matter what happens with the stakes, if we are going to rob the bank, we do it tomorrow.

R: Deal.

The two shake hands.

R: You still haven't explained why any of this presents a problem for my epistem—

H: Who is this guy?

R: Doesn't look like a cop.

A tall, heavy set, and sharply dressed man approaches the El Camino.

R: May we help you sir?

Big Guy: I think you've done enough.

R: Have we met?

BG: No. But I believe you've had business with one of my associates. Or I suppose I should say *former* associates. I'm The Big Guy.

H: Uh-oh.

R: Nice to meet you.

BG: Ordinarily, someone who dispatches an associate of mine without my blessing ends up joining him in a hole. But you caught me in a good mood.

R: Lot of that going around.

BG: See the Caddy over there?

R: Nice.

BG: I was waiting in it.

The Big Guy opens his jacket exposing a large pistol hanging from a shoulder holster.

BG: My little friend here was just minutes away from doing the very same thing your little friend there ended up doing. That's why I'm cutting you gals a break. You did me a favor. The Gooch was no good. I knew today was his day.

R: Understandable. Can't have members of The Syndicate putting around in Camrys.

BG: One of my tow trucks will be transporting that off to the scrap yard. Along with its occupant. The crusher needs a snack.

R: Good. But with all due respect sir, I gotta say if your reason for thinking The Gooch would check out today was that *you* would be the one who whacks him, then you were incorrect to say that you *knew* today was his day.

BG: What?

R: It's like this. Suppose Smith works in your office. Now I know you guys don't really have offices. It's more like a dirty room in the back of some strip club with a pool table and a little bar. But forget about that. Suppose Smith says he owns a Ford, you've seen him driving a Ford and he's even waved around some Ford title papers. Naturally, you believe that Smith owns a Ford and therefore somebody in your office owns a Ford. But suppose that's a hoax. It's a rental. But there's this other guy Jones who really does ow—

BG: I don't have time for this. And I don't deal in hypotheticals.

R: So if I were to ask you a hypothetical question, you wouldn't answer it?

BG: Before you two go thinking you're outta trouble completely, know that I'm aware of that rather large debt you had with our recently departed friend. That goes to me now. And I plan to collect. Soon.

R: No problem. We had an appointment with him at the usual place on Sunday. Before my wife canceled it that is. How about we meet then?

BG: I know the place. But I'm gonna need it tomorrow afternoon. 5 pm. And don't forget to bring along this nice '69 Elco and plenty of quarters. You'll be taking the bus home. I'll be taking your Chevy to cover the cost of me cleaning up the mess you left here in the parking lot.

The Big Guy heads back toward his Caddy.

R: Now that is a suit. Good thing your piece is nice and warmed up. We got us a bank to rob. Let's do this!

H: What?

R: You heard the guy. He needs the money tomorrow or we end up going through the crusher with The Gooch. And I'll be damned if my last ride on earth's gonna be in a Camry. I don't see why The Big Guy has to take the El Camino to cover the cleanup. He was about to do the same thing you did. There'd've been cleanup either way. But it is impressive to see a top guy do his own wet work for a change. Gotta respect that. I wonder if he works on that Caddy himself too. And hey, maybe this bank job will give us enough money to cover the debt *and* get another car! I've had my eye on Fred's big block T.A. for a while now. Wonder what he'd take for it.

H: Are you insane?

R: Says the person who just offed a guy in a parking lot to prove a philosophical point. Still waiting to hear what the point was by the way. Now I know the weight to horsepower ratio on a Bandit isn't so great but you gotta admit any two-door coupe with a 6.6 is totally badass. Some people think the decals are gaudy. I say of course they are. That's the whole point!

H: I don't want to talk about cars, Rosana. What about the resolution we made?

R: The what?

H: Back before The Big Guy came over, we resolved that if the stakes went back up and we had to hit the bank, we'd do it tomorrow. We both agreed that was a rational resolution to make. The stakes went up but now you're saying we gotta rob the bank today. What about our agreement? We had a deal.

R: Oh yeah, the deal. We made the deal when we took ourselves to know that the bank will be open tomorrow. We don't know that anymore. The stakes are way too high. If we come back tomorrow and this place isn't open, we aren't going to be able to get the money and we'll find ourselves stuffed into a suitcase sized Toyota before sundown. Now if it is in fact true that the bank will be open tomorrow, then it was rational for us to make that resolution. But it's not rational for us to stick to it because we don't know whether the basic presupposition of it was correct.

H: We shook on it.

R: Yeah I know we shook on it. But when we shook on it we took ourselves to know that the bank will be open tomorrow. But that might've been wrong. After all, looks like I was wrong when I said The Gooch is a poser. "Was" I mean. Anyways, if we were wrong to think the bank'll be open tomorrow and we stick to our little resolution, we're dead.

H: Didn't Socrates say you should keep your just agreements?[6]

R: Yep. And Socrates was right—in general. But he was wrong to think you should always keep a just agreement. There's an exception when your own life depends on it. Sure, he had an agreement with the Laws but as soon as sticking to that agreement meant he had to die for something he didn't even do, he should've broke the agreement and busted out. That's what I would've done. Same thing's going on here. I can't stick to an agreement on something my life depends on unless I know that I made the agreement rationally. I don't know that unless I know that my belief that the bank will be open tomorrow constituted knowledge at the time I made the agreement. And now I don't know that the bank will be open tomorrow because too much turns on it. And if I don't know it now I can't know that I knew it then. So the agreement is void.

H: That is absolutely ridiculous.

R: I don't see why. If you have a serious objection to the pragmatic encroachment thesis, I'm happy to hear it but you can't just sit there and call it ridiculous and expect me to be—

H: Hey look there's no line up there anymore.

R: Dammit.

H: What?

R: Look at the clock. It's 5:03. We can't hit the bank now. It's closed. We've been out here jawing over an hour. What are we gonna do now?

H: It'll be open tomorrow.

R: You don't know that.

H: Why not? Doesn't make a difference now.

R: I'm hungry.

> Is it ridiculous? Or was it a mistake for Rosana to make the agreement in the first place?

---

6   See Plato's "Crito," in *The Apology and Related Dialogues*, Cathal Woods and Ryan Pack (trans.) (Peterborough: Broadview P, 2016).

H: Denny's?

R: Okay. I kinda got a craving for some nachos.

H: Do they serve those there?

R: I don't know.

H: Doesn't matter.

R: Let's go.

H: I'm putting something else on the radio.

The Problem of Disagreement
My Dinner with Ling

People disagree. This is sometimes attributable to one of the parties having more information than the other. Sometimes disagreements happen because people are prone to irrationality or careless thinking or intellectual dishonesty. More philosophically interesting cases of disagreement, however, involve people who are *epistemic peers* of one another. Suppose two people are equally well informed about a certain issue, share all the same evidence, and exhibit all of the cognitive virtues to the same degree—they are equally rational, honest, thoughtful, and so on. But they still disagree. What is the rational response to this sort of disagreement?

The following example from David Christensen helps make the problem concrete.

> Suppose that five of us go out to dinner. It's time to pay the check, so the question we're interested in is how much we each owe. We can all see the bill total clearly, we all agree to give a 20 per cent tip, and we further agree to split the whole cost evenly, not worrying over who asked for imported water, or skipped dessert, or drank more of the wine. I do the math in my head and become highly confident that our shares are $43 each. Meanwhile, my friend does the math in her head and becomes highly confident that our shares are $45 each. How should I react, upon learning of her belief?[1]

---

1 David Christensen, "The Epistemology of Disagreement: The Good News," *The Philosophical Review* 116(2): 187–217 (2007).

There are a range of answers to this question. It is common to view them as being of two types: conciliatory and steadfast. The conciliatory approach says that when you find yourself in disagreement with an epistemic peer over a proposition P, the rational response is for both parties to reduce their confidence in P. In its simplest form, the conciliatory view says that the rational response to peer disagreement is for both parties to suspend judgment.

The way some understand it, the conciliatory view sees the existence of peer disagreement as an epistemic defeater for both parties.[2] In the above example, the fact that my peer performed a calculation and arrived at the result that we each owe 45 dollars serves as a defeater for my belief that we each owe 43 dollars rendering it unjustified. Likewise, the fact that my calculation differs from hers defeats her belief about what we owe. Thus we should both either suspend judgment or at least become significantly less confident about our totals than we were prior to the disagreement. This kind of approach is also called an "equal weight" view on disagreement; the beliefs of one's epistemic peers ought to carry as much force as one's own.[3]

Steadfast views of disagreement, on the other hand, hold that one need not suspend judgment or significantly reduce confidence upon learning that a peer disagrees. It can be rational to stay put. One kind of motivation for a steadfast approach is that conciliatory views threaten to leave us with a fairly wide-ranging form of skepticism. Consider the present state of philosophy. Some (but not all) think that professional philosophers can be viewed as epistemic peers of one another.[4] Yet, as everyone knows, there is a great deal of disagreement among them. So, one might conclude, the conciliatory view entails that one cannot be very confident at all when it comes to matters philosophical.

That presents a particularly sticky problem for the conciliatory view of disagreement because that view is itself a philosophical position over which there is disagreement. For this reason, it has been said that the conciliatory view is self-refuting; anyone who holds it is committed to giving it up or, at least, not being very confident about it.[5]

---

2   See Clayton Littlejohn's "Disagreement and Defeat," in *Disagreement and Skepticism*, Diego E. Machuca (ed.) (New York: Routledge, 2013).
3   Defenses of conciliatory views can be found in Richard Feldman's "Respecting the Evidence," *Philosophical Perspectives* 19: 95–119 (2005) and Adam Elga's "Reflection and Disagreement," *Noûs* 41: 478–502 (2007).
4   Thomas Grundman criticizes this idea in "Doubts about Philosophy? The Alleged Challenge from Disagreement," in *Knowledge, Virtue, and Action. Essays on Putting Epistemic Virtues to Work*, Tim Henning and David P. Schweikard (eds.) (New York: Routledge, 2013).
5   For a response to this kind of criticism see Jonathan Matheson's "Are Conciliatory Views of Disagreement Self-Defeating?," *Social Epistemology* 29(3): 145–59 (2015).

Part of the issue between different accounts of disagreement is over whether and to what extent evidence is "permissive." Can a given body of evidence allow for conflicting attitudes toward the same proposition to be equally justified? Suppose that a body of evidence *e* is relevant to some proposition P. One might think that *e* can only justify one unique attitude toward P. In other words, anyone who possesses evidence *e* and no other relevant evidence must either believe that P (in the case where the *e* is sufficient to justify P) disbelieve P (in the case where *e* suffices to justify believing Not-P) or suspend judgment (in the case where *e* is inconclusive). Insofar as steadfast views allow that both parties to a peer disagreement can be rational in maintaining different levels of confidence, proponents of those views tend to reject the idea that a given body of evidence can rationally justify only one attitude.[6]

Most responses to this problem are symmetrical. In other words, it is assumed that the rational response to peer disagreement—whether it is to reduce or maintain one's confidence concerning P—is the same for all parties. But, according to what has come to be called the "right reasons" view, the rational response to peer disagreement will depend on whether one reasoned correctly in the first place. In the example above, assume one person calculated correctly and the other got it wrong. According to the right reasons view, it's rational for the person who reasoned correctly to remain steadfast and the mistaken person should be conciliatory.[7]

The focus of this chapter is a dispute over how to split up the check after supper that blossoms into a disagreement about how one ought to respond to disagreement. One party is partial to the conciliatory view and another is a proponent of the right reasons view. The philosophical main course is preceded by an appetizer discussion on the epistemological implications of different ideas about the nature of consciousness and linguistic understanding.

June: [*voice over as a woman walks down a city street*] The life of the philosopher ain't easy. Epictetus was right. You shouldn't talk philosophy with non-philosophers. But he bungled the reason. It's not because you might end up saying something stupid. It's because the other guy definitely will. And you'll have to listen to it. But once in a while, I meet somebody outside the thought biz worth talking to. Take my buddy Ling. We met in China when I was over

---

6 Gideon Rosen criticizes the idea that there can be only one rational response to a given body of evidence in "Nominalism, Naturalism, Epistemic Relativism," *Philosophical Perspectives* 15: 69–91 (2001). An overview of the arguments on this issue can be found in Matthew Kopec and Michael Titelbaum's "The Uniqueness Thesis," *Philosophy Compass* 11(4): 189–200 (2016).
7 Thomas Kelly defends this sort of view in "The Epistemic Significance of Disagreement," in *Oxford Studies in Epistemology Volume 1*, John Hawthorne and Tamar Szabo Gendler (eds.) (Oxford: Oxford UP, 2005).

there about 15 years ago. Ling's a computer scientist by trade. And he loves philosophy. He's almost always wrong but I enjoy talking to him if only as a reminder of the value and correctness of my own ideas. I was delighted when he called me up out of the blue to tell me he was in town and invited me to supper. But at the same time, I was also a bit apprehensive. Ling doesn't speak any English. Not a word of it. And I haven't traveled in a while. So my Chinese is pretty rusty. In fact, I'm not even sure I got the address of the restaurant right when we spoke over the phone. I hope I still have the skills to keep up with the kind of stimulating conversation I know he'll want to have.

June opens the door of a restaurant, enters, and approaches the host.

J: I think I'm supposed to meet a friend here?

Host: Follow me.

The host leads June to a two-top table in the rear of the restaurant. On one side of the table, across from the empty chair, is a large black box on wheels, approximately four feet high and two and half feet wide. On the side of the box that faces the table, there is a horizontal slot near the top. Just above that, a lens and speaker are attached. Robotic arms extend from the unit's sides.

J: There must be a mistake. I'm supposed to eat dinner with a guy named Ling. Not a paper shredder on wheels.

The host smiles and returns to the front of the restaurant as a voice emanates from the speaker atop the box.

The Box: Something came up and Ling couldn't make it, June. So he sent me in his place—along with his apologies. I am one of Ling's colleagues from the PRC Artificial Intelligence and Robotics Institute. We're in town for a big conference.

J: You mean there's a person inside there?

B: Yep. Just call me The Box for now.

J: Okay, Mr. Box. May I ask why somebody would sit inside a trash can at dinner instead of at the table like a normal person?

B: I'm very shy and kind of a messy eater. Speaking of eating, would you care to sit down?

J: This is all kind of weird but I'm hungry. And I do love sushi. Why not?

J: [*voice over*] It was a very enjoyable supper—once I got over the strangeness of it all. I was relieved my companion spoke English so I didn't have to pull my Chinese from the mothballs. The Box couldn't handle the chopsticks too well with those robotic pincers on the ends of its arms. I noted how in Japan it's considered perfectly okay to eat nigiri with your hands—or hooks if that's all you have. I said it wouldn't bother me if The Box ate the sashimi that way too even though that's not normally done. Once the rules were clear, The Box started shoving slabs of fish into the slot one after the other. With each piece I would hear the motor on the shredder humming away as the internal blades destroyed the stuff. For some tasks, the pincers weren't very efficient. At one point, I asked The Box to pass the soy sauce and ended up with it all over my lap. Although there were often long pauses, the conversation was better than I thought it would be. It reminded me of the kinds of philosophical discussions I used to have with Ling. The Box had a lot to say but was thoroughly confused. If everyone would just read my articles on these topics, humanity would finally start to progress. I told The Box to give me an email address so I could send a link to my webpage. I need to get my download count up so I'll have something to show to the Associate Dean's productivity committee next week. By the time the seaweed salad was all gone, I was ready to wrap it up. I caught the waitress's eye and played the air pen so she'd bring the check.

J: I'm sorry Ling couldn't make it but I had a nice time tonight. Maybe the three of us can hook up before you head back east.

B: Great idea. But there's something I need to tell you.

J: Oh yeah? What?

B: It's me.

J: Who else would you be but you? That's a performative tautology like "I'm here" or "Listen up." You know, you'd do well to read my 2007 article in—

B: No June. It's me. Ling.

J: Ling?

B: Yeah. I fooled you. I'm in the man in The Box. This unit is a mobile computing device we've been developing at The Institute for the last 15 years. The project was my idea. You were the one who inspired me.

J: I've been known to have that effect on people. How's it work?

B: When you talk, there's a mic that picks up the sound and what you said appears in front of me on a screen in English text.

J: So Ling has learned to read English?

B: No. I still don't understand any English at all. But I have a tablet in here that gives me access to a vast electronic library. The tablet provides a set of instructions that tell me how to respond to the sentences on the screen.

J: So my English utterances are being translated into Chinese and then back into English?

B: No. The instructions only give me strings of English letters corresponding to what you said—the "inputs." The instructions direct me to produce a set of English letters in response—the "outputs." Then, here's what I do. I punch those English letters on my keypad. The computer makes the speaker up there generate a sound designed to mimic a human voice talking in English corresponding to the sentences I just entered.

J: I was wondering about that accent.

B: The first model had a more robotic voice but legal got worried Hawking might sue us. So we changed it.

J: These instructions, they contain every sentence I've uttered? And they tell you what English sentence to punch out in response?

B: Yep. In fact, the instructions contain directions on what to key in for every possible sentence you could utter.

J: That's a lotta instructions. You must be one fast reader.

B: I'm not reading. How could I? It's all in English. I'm just recognizing shapes. What you say is spelled out on the screen. Then I match those letter shapes to my instructions on the tablet. There is an arrow that directs me on what keys to hit in response. But none of the words mean anything to me.[8]

J: I guess you're no slouch of a typist either.

B: The point is I'm not really conversing with you. How could I? I don't speak English. I'm just manipulating what are to me completely meaningless symbols. In fact, I can't even see anything outside the box.

J: Is that why you dropped the soy sauce?

---

8   The Box is an example of what philosophers call a Chinese Room. That idea was first hatched in John Searle's famous paper "Minds, Brains and Programs," *Behavioral and Brain Sciences* 3(3): 417–57 (1980). A good and very short introduction to the topic can be found in the

B: Sorry about that. The pincers are just prototypes. My team doesn't handle that. But I did work on the light sensor you see up there next to the speaker. The arms and pincers are controlled by a set of dials and switches in here. The sensor receives information from the environment and then it provides me with another set of instructions on which dials to turn and which switches to flip. Additional software allows the different subsystems to interact and produce instructions that will appear coherent to an observer. But other than the instruction screens that tell me what buttons to push and dials to turn, I can't see anything from in here.

J: Not even the shredded tuna?

B: Is that what keeps falling on my head?

J: I'm not getting why you need a person in there. The person is just matching characters and then following a pre-existing set of instructions. But if you already have instructions on how to swap English sentences for other English sentences, why not wire the thing up to do all that automatically? Why do you need a human to do it? Is labor really that cheap over there?

B: It is absolutely essential that I am in The Box, June.

J: Why?

B: You might not remember. When we first met, we had a long discussion about consciousness, specifically, the nature of linguistic understanding.

J: Sounds like one worth forgetting.

B: You were defending the Strong Artificial Intelligence Program and claiming we could one day build a digital computer that could understand a natural language because, according to you, there is nothing to linguistic understanding other than symbol manipulation.

J: That's true. So I must've said it. If a machine can pass the Turing Test, in other words, if a machine can convince a human that it is talking to another human rather than a computer, then that computer is capable of thinking. I suspect Alan Turing took his test to be just a good *indicator* of thought. But I take it constitutively—a machine that passes the Turing Test *is* understanding what is being said and is therefore thinking.

B: Well, I disagreed with you June. And I still do.

YouTube video "60 Second Adventures in Thought: The Chinese Room." A thorough overview of the philosophical issues can be found in David Cole's entry "The Chinese Room Argument" in the *Stanford Encyclopedia of Philosophy* https://plato.stanford.edu/entries/chinese-room/ Some take this sort of example to show that a digital computer is not capable of linguistic understanding and, therefore, not capable of thought.

J: Always a mistake.

B: From that point on, I knew what I needed to do to. I would build a machine that could pass the Turing Test but for which it would be obvious that there was no understanding taking place. And I have done it. I have passed the Turing Test but I do not speak any English at all. Now you must admit you were wrong! Admit it!

J: Why would I do that?

B: Because I don't speak English. Yet, I fooled you!

J: Ling doesn't speak English. But that's not the issue.

B: What do you mean that's not the issue?

J: The question is whether a digital computer is capable of understanding a human language. And yes The Box is in essence a digital computer. But Ling is just a *part* of that computer. Ling doesn't understand English. But so what? That's like saying the keyboard on a computer doesn't understand things. Of course the keyboard doesn't understand. The question is whether *the computer* understands. And the keyboard is just one part of it. Or, in a human subject, the question is not whether some *part of my brain* thinks and understands but whether *I* do.[9]

B: Didn't Bertrand Russell say all you ever see is part of your own brain?

J: Yep.[10] And his argument applies to any other sensory modality. That reminds me: part of my brain tasted a little off when I was eating that sea urchin. I hope it wasn't spoiled. Anyways, it's not about whether Ling understands English but whether *The Box* does. And that's obvious. Not only can The Box pass the Turing Test, it can even pass the soy sauce! Sort of.

B: I said I was sorry. Passing bottles across a table is a task humans take for granted but it's very difficult to build a robot that can do it.

J: Harder than getting it to understand a natural language evidently. And speaking of passing things, I think that sea urchin is getting to me. I hope the waitress brings the check soon.

B: So you honestly think a trash can can understand?

---

9   This is called the "Systems Reply" to the Chinese Room argument.
10 "I should say that what the physiologist sees when he looks at a brain is part of his own brain, not part of the brain he is examining." Bertrand Russell, *The Analysis of Matter* (New York: Dover, 1954 [1927]), 383.

J: Not the ones you see by the curb. But you're one unique bin. You make a good philosophical point too. It's the opposite of the point you were supposed to prove. But that happens in philosophy. Just look at the umpteen refutations of skepticism out there. The Box proves computers can think. I already knew that of course but this might help the lesser minds out there.

B: I don't understand English but The Box does? That's completely absurd!

J: Why?

B: Because I'm the only biological organism in here. The rest of it is just plastic and metal. Nothing other than me in here even has a brain. So if I don't understand English, The Box certainly doesn't either.

J: I disagree. The Box is a brain—albeit an artificial one. But brains are like bait. And artificial bait is still bait. Speaking of bait, are you going to shred that last bit of mackerel? I need to settle my stomach.

B: Is a decoy mackerel still a mackerel? And lemme ask you this. What if it turned out that you opened up The Box and nobody's home? It's just wires and computer chips and stuff. In other words, what if we built this thing as you said we should have, so that my job in here is fully automated? Would you still say The Box understands?

J: Sure. Why wouldn't I? You seem to be assuming that consciousness requires brain matter. But what if you opened up my head and found no brain matter, just wires and computer processors and stuff? There's a sticker in there with a wiring diagram, like the ones they put on household appliances, and you can see I work just like a digital computer.

B: Then I'd conclude that you were a robot incapable of thinking—that you had only been simulating thought all this time.

J: And I should do the same if I opened up my friend Ling's head and found just a bunch of wires? I should conclude that Ling is not capable of understanding anything? Even Chinese?

B: Sure but that won't happen. I understand Chinese.

J: And what should I do if it happens to me? I've never had a CAT scan or anything like that. So if I get into a car wreck or something and my head splits open and a bunch of wires fall out, I should conclude that I don't understand English?

B: For starters, if you're just a digital computer, you aren't capable of thought. So you can't *conclude* anything. Second, you know through introspection that you are a conscious being who understands English.

In its original form, the Chinese Room thought experiment is told from the perspective of a native English speaker inside the room who does not understand Chinese but trades Chinese symbols for other Chinese symbols. How, if at all, does imagining the example from June's point of view affect the argument?

> June's argument here moves quickly. What are her assumptions? Are any of them dubious?

> Could one agree that consciousness requires brain matter and yet also reject June's argument here?

J: But it's possible I'm just wires and chips upstairs. I could learn that I don't have a biological brain. But I couldn't learn that I'm incapable of thinking. Therefore, biological brains are not necessary for consciousness.

B: Yes they are. And since they are, you couldn't learn that you don't have one.

J: Ah, so we have yet another refutation of skepticism about the physical world: I think. Therefore, I have a brain.

B: I'm fine with that. But maybe I overstated things by implying that biological brains are necessary for conscious thought. It's more a matter of degree. You know that you have a brain. And you know that your brain is responsible for your mental states. You know that other humans have brains too. And when you see them exhibiting the kinds of behaviors you know are caused by mental events in your own case, you can infer that these other beings have similar causes for their behavior. Like effects are preceded by like causes. Now, the less similar a being is to you, the more skeptical you should be of its capacity for conscious thought. If you meet a being with no brain matter at all, just wires and chips and stuff, you have a very good reason to think it might just be mimicking consciousness. In other words, the less like you the other being is, the bigger the problem of other minds gets.[11]

J: So I should think that men are less likely to have minds than women? And what should the boys think about me? And like I said, it could turn out that I'm the one that has wires and chips and whatnot inside. And if I were to find out that that is actually the case, by your own argument, I should conclude that brain-endowed humans are much less likely to be conscious than I am.

B: But you know you have a brain.

J: Maybe. But think about it from the point of view of the alternative type of box you mentioned earlier—the one where there is not a man inside because his job has been fully automated. That Box, quite obviously, is capable of thinking. So by your argument, assuming I do in fact have a normal human brain, that box should be skeptical of *my* ability to think. In fact that box should regard the very idea of a human mind with suspicion because—[12]

Waitress: I'll take this up as soon as you guys are ready.

The waitress drops off the check.

---

11 Compare John Searle's "Breaking the Hold: Silicon Brains, Conscious Robots, and Other Minds," in *The Nature of Consciousness*, Owen Flanagan, Ned Block, and Guven Guzeldere (eds.) (Cambridge, MA: MIT P, 1997).

12 June's thought here is similar to the one presented in Terry Bisson's "They're Made Out of Meat," first published in the April 1991 issue of *OMNI*.

J: Great. Okay, you shredded way more sushi than me but I'll let that slide. Divvying up our shares equally, that comes to—

B: Before we do that, let me ask you one more thing June. The simulated answers coming from the speaker are written from the point of view of me, Ling. For example, earlier the noise "I don't understand English" emanated from the speaker. You're convinced that you've been talking to someone who understands English. But you know I, Ling, do not. So who do you think you've been talking to?

J: After you revealed how The Box works, I noticed how some of your answers presupposed that Ling was doing the talking. But I took that to be just a glitch in the programming so I ignored it because of course I know Ling doesn't speak English. When you make the first-person utterance "*I* don't understand English" what you say is false. *Ling* doesn't understand English but The Box does and that's who's talking. Like I said before, Ling is just a part of The Box. What holds for the whole does not necessarily hold for all of its parts.

B: That's true.

J: But not every word of that is true. Ever notice when people say that? "What I said is true. Every word of it!" What you said might be true but that doesn't mean every word is. Why would it? That's just the fallacy of division—a fallacy, by the way, that you committed when you took that fact that Ling doesn't understand English to show The Box doesn't. Furthermore, it makes no sense to say a word is true. Only complete statements can be true. You also hear people say, "I believe every word of what he said!" How do you believe a word? I have a forthcoming article on this I'd be happy to email—

B: Okay, getting back to splitting up the check here.

J: Yes. The service was outstanding. So with a 12% tip that comes to ...

B: 45 each.

J: [*speaking simultaneously with The Box*] 43 each. What did you say?

B: Our shares come to 45 each.

J: No, they come to 43 each.

B: Looks like we've got another disagreement. Quite perplexing.

J: Nothing perplexing about it. It's obvious who's wrong.

B: It is? You performed a calculation that gives you a reason to think the bill is 43 dollars each. But now you are aware that I did the same thing and arrived at a different result. You've got some reason to think we each owe 43 dollars and some reason to think that's wrong. Along the same lines, I've got some reason to think our shares come to 45 dollars and some reason to think they don't. What is the rational response?

J: Let's look at the check again and I'll show you where you made the mistake.

Before June can grab the check, The Box snatches it with its metal pincers and feeds it into the slot. The shredder motor hums as the check is torn to ribbons.

J: What'd you do that for?

B: Because I want you to consider the question June. You are not going to budge in your dogmatic commitment to the idea that computers can think but perhaps progress can be made here. How should you react to our disagreement? Should you continue to believe that we each owe 43 dollars? Or should you back off? And what should I do?

J: What should you do?

B: Yeah. Should I continue to think we each owe 45 or should I give that belief up?

J: I thought you thought you didn't think at all.

B: I'm speech-simulating with the vulgar for now so you can focus on this other issue. What is the proper response to our disagreement?

J: I'm right and you're wrong. I'd prove it to you if you hadn't destroyed the check. In any event, we each owe 43 dollars. That's what I'm going to believe.

B: I could say the same to you. I could say that *I* am right and *you* are wrong.

J: You could say that. But when I say it, it's true.

B: I could say that too. How can you be so sure you are right and I am wrong rather than the other way around?

J: How do I know I'm right? Because we each owe 43 dollars not 45, just like I said.

B: That is a blatantly question begging dismissal of the evidence.[13] The fact that I arrived at a different result gives you evidence that you made a mistake in your calculation. Unless you have an independent reason for thinking you

---

13 David Christensen, "Disagreement, Question-Begging and Epistemic Self-Criticism," *Philosophers' Imprint* 11(6) (2011).

are right and I am wrong, it isn't rational for you to maintain your belief that our shares came to 43 dollars. Think of it this way. I have no reason to think any particular news channel in town is more reliable than any of the others regarding the weather. I watch Channel 12 and they report that the tropical storm has been upgraded to a hurricane. I flip over to Channel 7 and they say it hasn't. I say Channel 7 got it wrong—the storm has been upgraded. How do I know that? Because Channel 12 said so! But the fact that Channel 7 reported differently is evidence against Channel 12's report—and vice versa. To dismiss either report solely on the basis of the other is question-begging. And that's exactly what you are doing now. Your sole reason for thinking my calculation is wrong is that you arrived at a different one. But the fact that our calculations are different is a reason to doubt yours as well as mine.

J: Bad analogy. In the case of conflicting news reports, you have a third party who is fed testimony for P and then some more testimony for Not-P. But I divvied the bill myself. So I have first-hand knowledge of the facts. A more analogous case would be one where I'm the lead scientist at NOAA and know that the storm has been upgraded because I'm the one who upgraded it. In that case I would be in a position to dismiss any news report that said the storm hadn't been upgraded.

B: If you were the one who upgraded it and you remember doing so then yes, you would have an independent reason for preferring one report over the other. But in the case at hand, you have no *independent* evidence.

J: I've got all the evidence I need. My evidence deductively entails my conclusion that we each owe 43 dollars.

B: And it doesn't bother you that I could defend the result of my calculation with the very same argument? That I could say *I* have grounds that deductively entail that we each owe 45 dollars?

J: That's not the same argument. My argument is sound.

B: *My* argument is sound.

J: That's false.

B: It's false that it's false.

J: Sounds like you're in a loop. Maybe this will initiate your operating system's exit routine: You think the fact that I arrived at a different result gives you a reason to doubt yours. Why not save yourself 2 bucks, chip in 43 and we can get out of here? Or, heck, go ahead and put in 45 and I'll put in 43. The waitress can keep the extra.

B: But if you are wrong and I was right—which is just as likely to be the case—there won't be any extra. In fact, we'll be short two bucks and the waitress will have to eat the difference out of her tip. I'm not comfortable with that. How 'bout you pitch in 45?

J: I should pay a 2 dollar penalty for beating you at math?

The waitress approaches the table.

W: May I take the check?

J: My robot friend here seems have mistook it for a piece of nori. Perhaps you could bring us another copy?

W: Sorry but I can't. The computers have been shut down for the night. You guys have been here a long time. Everybody's gone home. Even the management. Once you guys paid, I was going to lock up and take the money with me and then put it in the drawer when I came in for the brunch shift tomorrow.

J: Do you remember what we had?

W: Yes but I don't remember the prices. Why don't I grab a menu and add everything up by hand?

B: Before you do that, perhaps you could help us settle a philosophical question.

J: 43 is the answer.

W: Oh, I love *Hitchhiker's Guide*!

B: You're a little off there.

J: Looks who's talking.

B: Simulating. June and I had a disagreement about how much we should each pay. So we were wondering what to think now.

J: My friend here is inclined toward the idea that when there is a disagreement between people one would antecedently think are equally likely to be correct, both parties should relinquish their positions and suspend judgment.

W: Ah, yes. The conciliatory view of disagreement. Did you know I was a philosophy major in college?

J: I assumed it when I saw you waiting tables.

W: It's a myth that philosophy majors can't earn a living. According to recent statistics, philosophy majors by mid-career out-earn people with degrees in business management, nursing, chemistry, political science, and a host of other allegedly more practical fields.[14] And how do you know I'm not waiting tables because I want to? Do you know much I pull down at this place?

J: Not everybody tips 12 per cent.

W: You got that right. And what do you do that's so great?

J: Relax. I was kidding around. I'm in the biz. Anyway, The Box thinks I should give up my belief that we each owe 43 dollars. But since I made the correct calculation there is no reason why I should do that. He should but not me.

W: That's what's called the right reasons view.

J: It's like they named it just for me.

W: Sounds like you and your robo-buddy have a disagreement about the check and another disagreement about disagreement.

B: You can call me Ling.

J: No you can't. Ling doesn't speak English. But that big box he's stuffed into does.

W: There's a person in there?

B: A person who does not speak English. But June thinks she's not talking to Ling but to some artificial yet intelligent being called The Box.

J: Intelligent up to a point anyway.

W: A Chinese room in a Japanese restaurant?

J: Isn't it an English room?

B: It's all Greek to me.

W: Wait a minute. If there's June and there's The Box and then there's this guy Ling inside the box, shouldn't the check be split three ways?

J: Ling didn't eat anything. But you make a good point when you said there are multiple disagreements here. So look Mr. Box—

B: My name is Ling. And I do not speak English.

---

14 See 2015–2016 College Pay Scale Report http://www.payscale.com/college-salary-report/majors-that-pay-you-back/bachelors?page=22#fullText.

J: Sure you do. But it's interesting your name is Ling. I have a friend named Ling. I think he's sitting inside you right now. But I'll call you Ling if that's what you prefer. The name suits you. I'd also like to point out that there's really no need to go back and refigure the check. I know what the amount was.

W: You remember what the bill came to?

J: No I don't. Once I figure up the tip and add it in I always remember the final amount but I tend to forget what the original total was.

B: The same thing happens to me.[15]

J: Another flaw in your programming.

B: It's intentional. My software includes a few forgetfulness algorithms designed to mimic the human mind. A computer with a perfect memory would likely fail the Turing Test.

J: Very clever. And your mathematical errors make you all the more personable. Me, I tend to remember only what's important. Like the fact that our shares were 43 each or 86 bucks combined—twelve per cent of which was the tip. So all you need to do is divide 86 by 1.12 and you get the result that the amount of the original pre-tip total was 76 dollars and 78 cents tax included. You can figure out the pre-tax total from there but I'll leave that as an exercise for you kids. In any event, now we all know what the original bill was: 76 dollars and 78 cents. So there's no need to go and add it up by hand. Now 12 per cent of that is 9 dollars and 22 cents—rounding up to the nearest penny of course.

W: You're very kind.

J: 76.78 plus 9.22 comes to 86 bucks. Divided evenly between us that means our shares come to 43 dollars—exactly what I said back when this whole conversation started. You see? I was right all long. Told you. Let's pay up and get out of here.

W: But Ling can make the same move. He can say your shares were 45 each and from there he can deduce a figure for the original bill and then add a tip, cut that amount in half and conclude that he was right all along.

B: And without the original bill in front of us, who knows which one of us is making the mistake?

---

15 Thomas Kelly reports that he also suffers from this problem in "Historical versus Current Time Slice Theories in Epistemology," in *Goldman and His Critics*, Brian McLaughlin and Hilary Kornblith (eds.) (New York: Wiley, forthcoming).

J: Since my initial calculation was correct, I don't need to remember what the original amount was because I'm in a position to deduce it. Since Ling's calculation was incorrect, he can't do that.

B: Another question begging dismissal of the evidence.

W: You seem to be assuming that there is only one unique rational attitude that a subject can take toward a proposition. But why couldn't it turn out that two different subjects who have the same evidence have differing but equally rational attitudes toward the same proposition?

B: If one party believes that P and another believes Not-P one of them is wrong.

W: One of them will have a false belief but I'm asking about rationality. Do we agree that it is possible to be rationally justified in believing something false?

B: Sure.

W: So why couldn't it turn out that, even though one of them is mistaken, both parties to a disagreement are justified in believing as they do?

B: We're talking about disagreements between epistemic peers. For both to be rationally justified, it would have to be that the totality of the evidence permits both belief in P and belief in Not-P. But that would mean a subject could flip back and forth between the two at whim without any change in rationality. That's absurd.[16]

W: I doubt it's psychologically possible to flip back and forth between opposing beliefs. But that wasn't what I was thinking about anyway. My idea was not that the evidence could permit a single subject to believe P and to believe Not-P equally well. Rather, the evidence might permit different attitudes across different subjects. Why couldn't two different subjects who possess the same evidence have differing but equally rational attitudes toward the same proposition?

B: Well if it can't happen for one subject why would it for two?

W: Because different subjects might have different epistemic goals.[17] Suppose for Subject A believing the truth is of primary importance while Subject B's

---

16 Roger White makes this sort of point in "Evidence Cannot Be Permissive," in *Contemporary Debates in Epistemology*, 2nd edition, Mattias Steup, John Turri, and Ernest Sosa (eds.) (New York: Wiley-Blackwell, 2013), 318.
17 Thomas Kelly offers this response to White's worry about arbitrary switching in "Evidence Can Be Permissive," in *Contemporary Debates in Epistemology*.

chief epistemic goal is the avoidance of error. Now suppose there's pretty decent but not overwhelming evidence in favor of a certain proposition.

B: What proposition?

W: Doesn't matter.

J: I really wonder if I'm getting sick.

W: Good. Let's use that. Suppose there's pretty good but not totally conclusive evidence for the proposition that June is about to get sick all over the table. Since our two subjects have different epistemic goals, the evidence might be enough to justify belief in Subject A—whose chief aim is to believe what's true. But that same evidence is not enough to justify belief in Subject B because Subject B wants above all else to avoid believing something false. B will suspend belief until further evidence comes up.

J: The evidence might be coming up any second.

W: Have some sake. The point is that different subjects can have different yet equally rational reactions to the same evidence if they have different epistemic goals.

B: But why couldn't a subject change goals at whim? Why couldn't A take believing the truth to be his primary goal at one time and then take avoiding error to be his primary goal a minute later and then switch back again? If he does then, at least in the kind of case you are thinking of, what it is rational for the subject to believe could also change with the wind.

W: I don't know if it's that easy to shift your fundamental epistemic goals around like that.

B: Why not? I can see why it might not be that easy to up and switch from believing P to believing Not-P because if you shift one belief you've gotta make some changes on whatever else is logically connected to it. But goals—which are a kind of value—can't be directly contradicted by the facts, right? Isn't that Hume's point?[18] So I don't see how this business about epistemic goals handles the problem.

J: That sake seems to be working for the time being. And Ling, you hold your ground pretty well for a conciliationist.

---

18 In the first section of Book III of *A Treatise on Human Understanding*, David Hume says that our "passions, volitions and actions" are not susceptible to any "agreement or disagreement" to matters of fact (New York: Penguin, 1985 [1739], 510).

B: I was only asking her some questions. And don't forget, I don't understand English, so I can't really disagree with either of you.

J: Anyway, I want to return to a point from earlier. Since philosophers disagree over the epistemology of disagreement, there is peer disagreement about how one ought to react to peer disagreement. So anyone who believes the conciliatory view of disagreement is committed to giving it up. If you believe it, you also believe that you shouldn't believe it. That's incoherent. But I guess that sort of philosophical mistake isn't too surprising coming from somebody who keeps insisting he doesn't speak English. In English.

B: I realize you don't approve of my philosophical views. But that remark is gratuitous.

J: "That remark is gratuitous" is gratuitous.

W: You could both use a lesson in gratuities

B: Nonetheless, I think you do have a point there, June. So okay, I hereby relinquish my commitment to the conciliatory view of disagreement.

J: You do?

B: Sure.

J: Am I the only one who sees a problem here?

W: The fact that the conciliatory view recommends its own rejection is not a problem.

J: How could that not be a problem?

W: Here's an analogy. Suppose some sort of simple utilitarian account of ethics is correct—so the morally correct action is the one that has the best overall consequences for all those affected. And suppose Ling Box here is well intentioned and wants to help others but he's also a bumbler—every time he tries to help somebody, he ends up making things worse.

J: Case in point: the soy sauce.

B: Are you going to bring that up all night?

W: The greater good would be best served if Ling avoided helping others out altogether and just focused on himself.

J: Because if he acts egoistically he minimizes the damage.

W: You got it.

> The Box also held its ground in debating June over whether computers can think. Is that consistent with The Box's commitment (assuming the box is capable of commitments) to the conciliatory approach to disagreement?

J: Are we factoring in the effect this will have on the dry-cleaning industry?

B: Give it a rest already.

W: And being a decent-hearted robot, Ling will feel much better and be more efficient at it if he thinks he's doing the right thing by looking out just for Numero Uno. The important thing to us humans is not actually being moral. That gets to be very inconvenient. What's most important is that we are able to think of ourselves as moral. That's what really makes people happy. I reckon it's the same for robots. In a case like this, the utilitarian theory would recommend that Ling abandon it in favor of ethical egoism.

J: That way everybody's happy. He's not screwing up anybody else's life and he gets to say he's a morally upstanding box.

W: But the fact that utilitarianism recommends that Ling reject it in favor of ethical egoism doesn't mean utilitarianism is false. It only means Ling shouldn't believe it. A view can recommend its own rejection without being false.[19] You see the analogy. The fact that the conciliatory view of disagreement recommends its own rejection does not make it false.[20]

J: But to make the analogy fit, we can't set it up so Ling is unaware that the world would be a better place if he were an egoist. After all, he is aware that the conciliatory view of disagreement seems to recommend its own rejection. So we'd have to imagine that Ling started off as a utilitarian and then made some calculations and realized that the greater good is best served by him adopting ethical egoism. And so he adopted ethical egoism *for that reason*. But then, after he rejects utilitarianism in favor of ethical egoism, what is Ling to make of his earlier conversion? Assuming he remembers why he switched—i.e., to serve the greater good—he can't as an egoist say it was for the right reason. So, from his later standpoint, he would have to look back at his own rejection of utilitarianism as wrong.

W: As long as ethical egoism says he's better off as an egoist than he is a utilitarian, and presumably it would, there's nothing incoherent about his final position.

J: Maybe. But what's Ling supposed to think of his giving up on his belief that we each owe 45 dollars now that he no longer endorses the conciliatory view of disagreement? And what is supposed to make of his giving up on

---

19 For more on self-effacing ethical theories see Derek Parfit's *Reasons and Persons* (New York: Oxford UP, 1984)
20 Jonathan Matheson makes this kind of point in "Are Conciliatory Views of Disagreement Self-Defeating?," *Social Epistemology* 29(2): 145–59 (2015).

the conciliatory view? He cannot regard these moves as rational because that would presuppose a view he says he no longer holds. So what is he going to say?

W: Why don't you ask him?

J: Good idea. Ling, you used to believe that we each owe 45 dollars. Then you gave that belief up because you believed that the rational response to peer disagreement is to suspend judgment.

B: Yep.

J: But then you learned that there is peer disagreement over what to do about peer disagreement. Some accept the conciliatory view, some reject it. So you gave up the conciliatory view of disagreement.

B: What else was I gonna do?

J: Exactly. What do you think right now of your previous changes of mind? Were they rational?

R: I don't know.

J: You don't know?

R: Yeah. I don't know whether it was rational for me to give up like that or not.

J: I'm beginning to reconsider whether you understand English.

W: Makes perfect sense to me. He can't say it was rational because that would commit him to the conciliatory view of disagreement. Since he holds no view at all about how one ought to react to disagreement, all he can say is that he doesn't know whether giving up was rational or not.

J: "I hereby suspend judgment on whether P because of disagreement. But now I don't know whether it is rational to suspend judgement because of disagreement." That's absurd.

W: I've met plenty of people who say they hold their religious beliefs on faith. This is a way of saying "I believe but I have no good evidence." In what sense is that "absurd"? And he's not *denying* that something he currently believes is rational. He is suspending judgment on whether some previous acts of suspending judgment were rational.

J: What are you going to do the next time you confront peer disagreement, Ling? Are you going to suspend judgment?

R: I don't know.

J: Of course not.

> The waitress is advocating what we might call an "externalist" interpretation of the conciliatory view of disagreement (and utilitarianism). On an "internalist" conception of that view, the subject who suspends judgment would need to be aware of why it is rational for him to do so. Which interpretation is better?

W: Sounds like a good answer to me. Like I said, the conciliatory view of disagreement might still be true even though Ling cannot rationally believe it. If he reacts to future peer disagreements by suspending judgment, then, on the conciliatory view, he is being rational even if he doesn't know it. To go back to our moral example, as long as egoist Ling keeps acting selfishly, he's maximizing the greatest good for the greatest number and therefore, assuming a simple utilitarian theory, he's doing the right thing even if he can't say why.

J: But Ling didn't just withhold judgment. He withheld judgment in response to a certain fact—the fact that he met a peer who disagreed. By doing that, he thereby commits himself to the view that it is rational to respond to disagreement in that way. If he continues to suspend judgment, he maintains that commitment. So, whether he admits it or not, his actions show that he still endorses the conciliatory view. And since there is disagreement about it, he's being incoherent.

W: The analogous view in ethics would say that whenever we do something we're effectively announcing that the act is morally permissible. That might sound attractive to some but I don't buy it. You can do things you know are wrong. By acting a certain way, you aren't thereby saying that this is how everyone should act. I don't buy the idea here either. To take an attitude toward a proposition, be it belief or suspension of judgment, is not necessarily to endorse that attitude as rational or as the way everybody ought to think. If he continues to suspend judgment in response to disagreement, that's not the same as judging that it is rational to do so. Nonetheless, it might be true that this is the rational way to respond to disagreement.

J: Ling doesn't know how he will or should react the next time he confronts a disagreeable peer. Sounds like you don't know what he's gonna do either. Let's find out. Here's an easy one, Ling. Is there a God?

B: Yes. Do we disagree about that too?

J: We'll get to me in a second. Do you regard our waitress—with all her training in philosophy—as an epistemic peer on this issue?

B: Sure.

J: Let's see whether you disagree with her. So what's your take on this whole God thing?

W: Agnostic. The arguments for theism and the arguments for atheism both fail. Nobody knows one way or the other.

B: I'd love to hear what you think is wrong with the ontological argument. I know Kant thought existence wasn't a property but, you see, that is irrelevant because the axioms of S—

J: I'm sure she's just as familiar as you are with the ontological argument, Kant's critique of it, the various systems of modal logic et cetera, et cetera.

W: What kind of waitress would I be if I weren't?

J: But you still disagree. So it appears we have a genuine peer disagreement here. You are a theist, she's an agnostic. What are you going to do?

B: I haven't decided.

J: Well before you do, note this. You can't react to this disagreement by recommending that everyone suspend judgment. She's already doing that. If you decide to move from believing in God to suspending judgment on the issue, you are just adopting her position. Even a plastic box shouldn't be that spineless. And, if you think everyone should suspend judgement, then she doesn't have to budge a bit even though she has a peer—namely, you—who disagrees. How's that fair? The conciliatory view falls apart in this kind of case.

W: No it doesn't.

J: Why not?

W: The most this case shows is that we need to move away from the all-or-nothing model of belief.[21] Rather than say that a subject does or doesn't believe that P, we should think in terms of the degree of confidence or credence the subject has toward the proposition. Credences are assigned a number between 1 and zero with zero being the lowest degree of confidence in a proposition, 1 being the highest, and the intermediate degrees of confidence falling in between. I've always found this kind of model more natural than the all-or-nothing conception of belief. As new evidence comes in, it doesn't bring about change in what or whether I believe so much as it changes how sure I am of various things. This sort of view respects the nuances in our attitudes in a way that the all or nothing model cannot. Rather than say Ling believes in God full stop, let's say he adopts a credence of 0.9 toward the proposition that God exists—meaning that he's very confident but, being philosophical, not absolutely certain. Being staunchly agnostic, I think it's basically 50–50 that there's a God. In other words, I assign the proposition that God exists a credence of 0.5. Now it is clear how the conciliatory view would apply. It would tell Ling

---

21 This is how Thomas Kelly responds to the problem June raises in "Disagreement and Higher-Order Evidence," in *Social Epistemology: Essential Readings*, Alvin Goldman and Dennis Whitcomb (eds.), (Oxford: Oxford UP, 2010).

and me to meet in the middle and settle our disagreement by each adopting a credence of 0.7 toward the proposition that God exists.

B: So on this model, the conciliatory view recommends that the parties to a peer disagreement take the average of their credences and believe the proposition in dispute to that degree.

W: That's a good enough way to think of it for now.[22] And you see how the problem June raises goes away. Neither of us is just staying put in response to the disagreement and neither of us is just spinelessly adopting the position of the other. The recommendation is that I should increase my confidence in the proposition that God exists because my peer says that I'm not as confident in it as I ought to be. And Ling should decrease his confidence in the proposition that God exists because he has a peer who says he is irrationally overconfident. But neither of us is expected to go all the way over to the other's original point of view. So, no problem.

J: Not so fast. Ling earlier asked what my own position on this is: I'm an atheist.

B: Why am I not surprised?

J: I give the proposition that God exists a 0.1. So what we've got here is a three-way disagreement. Ling believes the proposition that God exists to degree 0.9, you give it a 0.5, and I have almost no confidence in that proposition, 0.1. The proposal on the table is that we ought to resolve disagreements by having the parties involved assign a credence value equivalent to the arithmetic mean of the different credences of each of the disagreeing parties. But 0.9 plus 0.5 plus 0.1 divided by three is—

B: 0.5!

J: Good to see that your calculation algorithms are not completely broken Ling. But 0.5 is exactly where our waitress started. So here we have two parties just adopting the position of the third while that person gets to stay exactly where she was even though two of her peers say she is wrong. Even if we are thinking in terms of credences rather than all-or-nothing beliefs, the conciliatory view breaks down when we consider three party disagreements like the one we have here.

---

22 This method of settling disagreements by adopting the arithmetic mean of the disputant's credences may not be ultimately sustainable. For an overview of the reasons why, see David Christensen, "The Epistemology of Controversy," *Philosophy Compass* 4/5: 756–67 (2009).

W: I still don't see any problem. You have two peers—namely, Ling and me—who think you are irrationally underconfident in your belief about God. Ling has two peers—you and me—who think he is irrationally overconfident. So it makes sense to say you should increase your confidence a bit and he should decrease his a bit.

J: So Ling and I have to shift our confidence levels but your own position remains completely unaffected? Even though two of your peers disagree? How's that fair?

W: I have one peer telling me I am overconfident and another telling me I'm underconfident. Those two cancel each other out. I'm just right.

J: Except we're talking about God not porridge. Suppose we have a disagreement between three expert weight guessers at the county fair. One says I weigh 125 another says 135 and a third says 145. If we buy the idea that peer disagreement undermines belief, doesn't the guy in the middle have very good evidence against his estimate? Yes, there's one person saying it's too high and another saying it's too low. But so what? He still has two peers telling him he's wrong. And you have two peers telling you your credence level on God is wrong. Yes one says it's too high another says it's too low. But so what?

B: In the case of the three weight estimators, it sounds like the rational response is for all of them to suspend judgment until they can put you on the scale.

J: But if you do that in the God case, that's just agnosticism. And she's already there. So what's she supposed to do? Not change her mind at all? And what are we supposed to do? Just take up her side?

W: Your weight guesser example is irrelevant. There you have three people who believe three different and conflicting propositions. But here we're talking about different credence values for the same proposition. The credence value one has toward a proposition is not written into the content of that proposition, it is built into the attitude itself.

J: The point is that you have two peers telling you your attitude is off-kilter given the evidence. It doesn't matter that one thinks you are overconfident and another thinks you are underconfident.

W: I disagree. But here's another way to look at things. Perhaps I'm not even part of the disagreement between you two over God. Yours is an ontological dispute—one of you says God exists, the other says God doesn't exist. I hold no position in that debate. I'm only advocating an epistemological position. So maybe I should just stay out of it.

Who is right here, June or the waitress?

J: You're already in. You've advocated two epistemological claims: First, that theism is irrational and, second, that atheism is irrational. Theism and atheism also involve epistemological claims. Ling not only believes in God but also believes that it is rational to believe in God. And I not only think God does not exist, I think that it is rational to think that. So you are contradicting both of us.

W: Like I said before, not all believers believe it's rational to be a believer.

J: It might be true that your average everyday theist believes in God but doesn't have second-order beliefs about the rationality of that belief, but a theistic philosopher will. Ditto for the atheistic and agnostic philosophers. Each believes that his position is the rational one. That's why they all contradict one another at some level.

B: Then why not give up on all three?

J: That doesn't make any sense. You can't simultaneously give up on theism, atheism, and agnosticism all at once.

B: In a sense, you can. The waitress's agnosticism conflicts with both my (formerly held) theism and your atheism because it is part of her position that theism and atheism are both irrational. She also thinks it is rational for her to think that theism and atheism are irrational. And we reject that.

J: Yeah, so?

B: So I am envisioning a version of agnosticism even more extreme than hers. What if you withheld judgment not just on the question of whether God exists but also on the question of whether it is rational to withhold judgment on whether God exists?

J: Would you also withhold judgment on whether it is rational to withhold judgment on whether it is rational to withhold judgment on whether God exists?

B: Of course. And ditto all the way up. Call that view *deep agnosticism*. The position can be adapted to any proposition. To be deeply agnostic on whether P is to withhold judgment not only on P but also on 2nd, 3rd, and n-th order judgments about the rationality of this attitude. Applied to the God question, the deep agnostic withholds judgment on the proposition that God exists, on the proposition that it is rational to do that and on the proposition that it is rational to do *that*. And so on.

W: But then you'd have an infinite number of withholdings. How is that possible for a finite being?

> The three positions will also have some overlap. Fun exercise: draw up a Venn diagram mapping out the points where the theist, atheist, and agnostic philosopher agree and disagree on each of the following propositions. G: God exists; RG: It is rational to believe G; R-G: It is rational to believe R Not-G; RRG: It is rational to believe RG; RR-G: It is rational to believe R-G.

B: If you think of each of the withholdings as occurrent attitudes, it might not be. But you don't have to think of it that way. You believe grass is green. You also believe "grass is green" is true. And that "'grass is green' is true" is true. You can commit yourself to tacking on infinitely many "is trues" just by adding an "and so on." This is what the deep agnostic does. I suspend judgment on whether God exists and on whether it is rational to suspend judgment on whether God exists *and so on*. This way there is no threat of conflict with peers—or anyone else—at any level. Notice also that this view would avoid the problem of self-refutation that standard versions of the conciliatory view face.

J: How so?

W: The proponent of the conciliatory view, as that view is usually understood, runs into trouble because he judges that it is rational to suspend judgment in cases of peer disagreement. And thereby finds himself in disagreement with his steadfast peers. But a deeply agnostic approach to peer disagreement makes no higher order claim of rationality so it doesn't have that problem.

W: Sounds like the sort of position you find in ancient Pyrrhonian skeptics like Sextus Empiricus. He distinguished his variety of skepticism from both the Dogmatist—who claims to know the nature of things—and the Academic—who claims that such knowledge is impossible. His brand of skepticism is distinct in that it involves suspension of judgment on everything.

J: Everything except "appearances"—whatever those are.[23]

B: And it's no accident Sextus advanced this position largely by way of arguments from disagreement. The ancient skeptics were conciliationists.

J: But unlike our contemporary conciliationists, they took it all the way.

W: I see how the deep agnostic avoids some of the problems ordinarily faced by the conciliatory view of disagreement. But at what price? You end up with a very extreme version of skepticism.

B: I'm only applying the idea in cases of peer disagreement. So whether it is extremely skeptical or not will depend on how much genuine peer disagreement there is out there.

J: But can you really avoid making any epistemic judgments? It sounds like you are endorsing a certain plan—a plan to react to peer disagreement by suspending judgment and by suspending judgment on whether it is rational to do that and so on. But doesn't your endorsement of that plan involve a tacit

---

23 See Sextus Emipricus, *Outlines of Pyhhronism*, Julia Annas and David Barnes (trans.) (Cambridge: Cambridge UP, 2000).

epistemological judgment that this is the rational way to proceed? And won't you have peers who think your plan is stupid? And isn't that enough to make the same problems show up all over again? I'm also wondering if you can really stop the slide into total skepticism. You hope to do that by restricting your deeply agnostic approach to cases of peer disagreement. That will work only if you are clear on who is or is not your peer. But what if there is disagreement about that?[24]

B: I'd like to answer that but I should point out that a bunch of people are coming in through the front door. I thought the restaurant was closed. Is this a robbery?

W: Oh no. That's the brunch crew. Looks like we've been here all night. I guess I'll just go ahead and start my new shift. You guys never paid but if you're hungry, I can roll your tab over and you can order some more.

J: Sounds good. Let's get another boat and some more sake. And which way's the restroom?

J: [*voice over*] As I headed in the direction the waitress pointed, I reflected on how many philosophical mistakes she and Ling had made. Begging the question here, confusing necessary and sufficient conditions there. Then, when I opened the door of the restroom, I found someone was already in the stall. So I stood by the door and I told her all about my dinner with Ling.

---

24 As noted earlier, there is disagreement among philosophers over whether philosophers are epistemic peers of one another.

Yet Another Gettier Problem
Philip

The JTB Theory of knowledge says that S knows that P if and only if (a) S believes that P, (b) P is true, and (c) S is justified in believing that P. This seems to capture many of both the obvious cases of knowledge and the obvious cases of ignorance. But in 1963, Edmund Gettier published a now legendary three-page paper. By way of two examples, he convinced nearly everybody that the JTB Theory fails to provide a complete analysis.[1] One can believe that P on the basis of excellent evidence, be right, and yet not know.

The following is a Gettier-style example from Richard Feldman's *Epistemology*.

> Smith knows that Nogot, who works in his office, is driving a Ford, has Ford ownership papers, is generally honest, etc. On this basis he believes:
>
> 1. Nogot, who works in Smith's office, owns a Ford.
>
> Smith hears on the radio that a local Ford dealership is having a contest. Anyone who works in the same office as a Ford owner is eligible to enter a lottery, the winner receiving a Ford. Smith decides to apply, thinking he is eligible. After all, he thinks that (1) is true, so he concludes that:

---

[1] Edmund Gettier, "Is Justified True Belief Knowledge?," *Analysis* 23(6): 121–23 (1963). For an example of a philosopher unconvinced by Gettier, see Stephen Hetherington, "Knowing Failably," *Journal of Philosophy* 96(11): 565–87 (1999).

2. There is someone who works in (my) Smith's office who owns a Ford.

It turns out that Nogot is a Ford faker and (1) is false. However, (2) is true because some other person unknown to Smith, Havit, works in his office and owns a Ford.[2]

Smith believes on very good grounds that someone in his office owns a Ford. And in fact someone in his office owns a Ford. But, the thought is, he does not know it. So the JTB Theory does not provide sufficient conditions for knowledge.

Much of the subsequent history of epistemology (some would say too much of it) was devoted to attempting to develop an account of knowledge that can accommodate Gettier-style examples. This is what has come to be known as the Gettier problem.[3]

This chapter does not attempt to solve the Gettier problem. Instead it offers yet another Gettier-style example. But, as we shall see, this example is different and more complicated than the more familiar ones. Some in our story seem to think the situation presents a new epistemic paradox. Others are less impressed.

Ethan: Were you there with S yourself, Philip, when he got gettiered or did you hear of it from someone else?

Philip: I was there. As you know, S and I are both knowledge-workers in the same office.

E: How did such a careful reasoner as S manage to get gettiered?

P: Gettier never takes a wise man by surprise. He is always ready to get gettiered.[4]

---

2 Richard Feldman, *Epistemology* (Upper Saddle River, NJ: Prentice-Hall, 2003), 26.
3 For a discussion of the problem (and of the problem with the problem) see William G. Lycan, "On the Gettier Problem Problem," in *Epistemology Futures*, Stephen Hetherington (ed.) (Oxford: Oxford UP, 2006).
4 Michael Roth, in "The Wall and the Shield," *Philosophical Studies* 59(2): 137–57, 152 (1990), points out that, from the point of view of the subject, a Gettier case will "look and feel" just like a case of knowledge. Matthias Steup says that what distinguishes Gettier cases from corresponding cases of knowledge is always "hidden" from the subject in "In Defense of Internalism," in *The Theory of Knowledge*, Louis P. Pojman (ed.) (Belmont: Wadsworth, 1999), 377. William Lycan says that "from within one's own epistemic situation, one has no way of knowing whether or not one is being gettiered" (*Judgment and Justification* [Cambridge: Cambridge UP, 1988],

E: I wish you would be nice enough to tell us how it happened—if you have the time.

P: Certainly. Nothing gives me more joy than elucidating a gettier case. Our ability to take delight in labyrinthine tales of people who have justified true beliefs without knowledge is what separates us from the beasts and ethicists.

E: But what do you mean by being "gettiered," Philip? It seems that not everyone uses the term in the same way.

P: You are correct, Ethan. Knowledge-workers use the term in different ways. This has led to much confusion. I take a gettier case to be one where a subject forms a justified true belief that P and this belief is essentially grounded in at least one false assumption.[5]

E: I see. Then please tell me how S was gettiered.

P: The story originates with Richard who, as you know, is another esteemed knowledge-worker.

E: I am sorry to stop you so early, Philip. But there are numerous Richards in the knowledge trade. To which do you mean to refer?

P: Richard F.

E: I see.

P: Weeks earlier, Richard arrived at the knowledge office and announced that he had just purchased a 1971 Chevrolet Corvette. From that day on, Richard would arrive at the building each morning and do multiple laps through the parking lot so that the other knowledge-workers there could appreciate his wondrous vehicle. Richard would sound the car's horn repeatedly until everyone who had already arrived and was inside the building would come to the window and also admire his automobile. He wore to work each day a red silk jacket with the Corvette checkered flag logo stitched to the back. He changed his ringtone to play Prince's 1982 smash hit "Little Red Corvette." He even tacked the car's title to the wall of his cubicle and insisted that everyone who passed by read it.

E: It sounds like Richard wanted there to be no doubt about this Corvette.

---

131). I defend the opposite point of view in "I Know I Am Not Gettiered," *Analytic Philosophy* 54(4): 401–20 (2013).

5   I offer an argument for this way of understanding gettierization in "I Know I Am Not Gettiered." It is worth pointing out that the classic fake barn cases would not count as gettier cases under this way of understanding things.

P: And there was none. All of the knowledge-workers in the office arrived at the firm belief that Richard owns a Corvette.

E: Didn't he seem like a braggart?

P: He did. But being close friends of him, most of us were willing to forgive Richard's behavior. S, however, resented him. Many thought this was due to jealousy. S drives a Camry.

E: I see.

P: But S became delighted because of what happened one night when he was staying late in the office.

E: Why was S staying late?

P: Decades earlier, when S was still a young knowledge-worker, he wrote a paper on the New Riddle of Induction.[6] In that paper, S chose to designate 12am of July 17th 2015 as time *t*. S was so young and this time seemed so far away, S thought it would never come. But the unyielding march of time had now brought it before him. For this was the 16th day of July 2015. Thus S sat at his desk late that night frantically observing as many emeralds as he could before the fateful deadline passed.

E: Fascinating.

P: We are only beginning. Richard was also working late in the office. The building manager had announced that there would be a surprise fire drill that week. Richard had proven that this was impossible—unless the drill happened after the office was closed and everyone was home. That was the only time it could not be expected. So Richard sat waiting at his desk all night every night that week.[7]

E: Did Richard know S was there?

P: It did not seem so. But S saw Richard there. S chose not tell Richard that he too was working late. He did not even want to say hello because of his simmering resentment over Richard's ongoing automotive ostentation.

E: What happened that delighted S so much?

P: S overheard Richard making a phone call from his cubicle.

---

[6] See Nelson Goodman, *Fact, Fiction and Forecast* (Cambridge, MA: Harvard UP, 1955).

[7] For an overview of the paradox alluded to here, see Roy Sorensen's entry "Epistemic Paradoxes" in the *Stanford Encyclopedia of Philosophy* https://plato.stanford.edu/entries/epistemic-paradoxes/. I critique one proposed solution to it in "On a So-Called Solution to a Paradox," *Pacific Philosophical Quarterly* 97(2): 283–97 (2016).

"Hello. Impressive Car Rental?" Richard said. "This is Mr. F. I have some complaints about the Corvette I've been renting from you. First, one of the flip-up headlights keeps getting stuck. Second—"

E: It's a rental!

P: That is what S immediately suspected. But, as you mentioned, S is a careful reasoner. He wanted more proof. When Richard stepped out of the office to enjoy a cigarette, S seized the opportunity to sneak over to Richard's cubicle and investigate matters further. S leaned in and looked closely at the car title tacked to the cubicle wall. It appeared to be a copy generated from the office's own Xerox machine.

E: How could he tell what machine made the copy?

P: Copies made on the office Xerox always have a tell-tale thin dark line in the lower left corner. You see, in the previous year, there had been a Christmas party at the knowledge office. One of the knowledge-workers—I have sworn not to say which—cracked the glass on the copy machine when he sat upon it in an effort to test experimentally Berkeley's theory that *esse* is *percipi*.

E: There does not exist a party resembling a knowledge-worker's party.

P: Upon further inspection, it appeared that Richard's name on the title had been typed over someone else's name on the original before the copy was made.

E: I've heard corrupted youth make fake identification cards in that manner. It's a fake car title!

P: It certainly looked that way. S was now highly confident that Richard had been merely *pretending* to own a Corvette. But just to make sure, S used his penknife to break into the locked drawer of Richard's desk.

E: It is a genuine lover of truth who will not permit even The Laws to impede him in his pursuit of what he most desires. What did S find in the drawer?

P: He found what appeared to be billing invoices from Impressive Car Rental. The paperwork documented that Richard had been renting a 1971 Corvette, license plate JTB-FU2—the very license plate everyone had seen on the Corvette Richard had been driving to work every day. Given this mountain of incriminating evidence, S concluded that Richard does not own that Corvette.

E: Did S tell any of the other knowledge-workers?

P: The next day at the office, in the coffee room, S reported the scandalous affair to Jones.

E: How did Jones react?

P: This is where the story takes its first interesting turn. Upon hearing S's story, Jones confessed to owning a Corvette himself. Jones told S that he inherited one from his grandfather. But Jones also thinks Corvettes are showy and inefficient so he is embarrassed to have one. But for sentimental reasons, he cannot part with it. Jones told S that he keeps his Corvette under a tarpaulin in his garage and he's never told anyone about it, until now. Jones asked S to keep this a secret because Richard and Smith had been pestering Jones and ridiculing him for his outspoken environmentalism—especially the "SAVE GAS! SAVE THE PLANET!" bumper stickers Jones plastered over every inch of his cubicle walls.

E: One always wants a confidant. But if Richard and Smith came to believe that Jones has a Corvette in his garage, they would call him a hypocrite and the ridicule would only increase.

P: Indeed.

So Jones said to Richard, "If you tell no one about this, I'll let you borrow my Corvette for the whole weekend."

E: I see where this is going, Philip. Just like the others, S believed someone in the office owns a Corvette because he believed, on very good evidence, that Richard owns a Corvette. Richard doesn't own a Corvette. It's a rental. But it is still true that someone in the office owns a Corvette because Jones owns a Corvette.

P: It would appear so.

E: But then I am very disappointed, Philip. This is an ordinary textbook gettier case. I am surprised that a knowledge-worker as experienced as S—someone who has been involved in many complex epistemological situations over so many decades—would have been gettiered in such a common manner. An example like this is hardly worth talking about.

P: If the story stopped here, Ethan you would be correct. But I have not finished. Later on, about midday, S found himself alone in the office. The other knowledge-workers had all said they were going to lunch. S chose to stay behind so that he could call some jewelers to see if they had obtained any shipments of blue emeralds that day. Of course, it had occurred to S that he and others in the office had been gettiered. S took a break from his research to reflect.

"I am glad I found out that Jones owns a Corvette," S thought to himself. "But others around here aren't so lucky. Take Smith. He believes, with good reason, that someone in the office owns a Corvette. It is true that someone in the office owns a Corvette. But Smith thinks it is Richard when really it is Jones. Smith is gettiered."

S then thought about how difficult the whole situation was.

"I could ungettier Smith by informing him of Richard's fakery and providing him with my new information about Jones," he mused, "but that would betray Jones's confidence and then he won't let me borrow his Corvette this weekend."

E: I understand. If you have to spend your Saturday in a Camry, you might as well just stay at work. What happened next?

P: At that moment, the building's security guard burst into the office.

"There's been an accident in the parking lot," he announced, "the big tree fell over and destroyed someone's car. Does anyone who works in this office own a Corvette?" Since he was there alone, S felt compelled to answer. But he could not say "No" without lying. And he felt that answering "Yes" would betray Jones's confidence especially if the security guard demanded to know who owned the Corvette.

E: He did promise not to tell *anyone*.

P: Indeed. So he devised a simple solution.

"I'll tell you this much," S said, "someone in this office is gettiered in his belief that someone in this office owns a Corvette."

E: Brilliant! The answer is truthful and gettierization is factive—one cannot be gettiered in his belief that P unless P is true. The information the security guard seeks is deducible from what S said. One cannot say he failed to provide an answer. But S can assume that a security guard would not know what it means to be gettiered. So he would have to look it up and this would afford S time to slip out of the office. Or perhaps the security guard would conclude S was speaking in riddles and just move on to the next office in the building. Either way, S answers the question and keeps his promise to Jones.

P: That was S's strategy. But he had miscalculated. The security guard, it turns out, was also a trained in the craft of knowledge-work.

E: It is the most versatile of all forms of education.

P: The security guard said to S, "I see. If someone is gettiered in his belief that someone in this office owns a Corvette, then it follows that someone in this office owns a Corvette. You have provided me with the information I sought. There must be some reason why you have flouted Grice's maxim of quantity and given me *more* information than I sought.[8] But I will respect your privacy by not inquiring further. I can now look at the parking pass registration slips and determine who the Corvette belongs to. Since I know it is someone from this office and not one of the other offices in the building, you have saved me a great deal of time. Good day sir!" S was surprised but pleased that he did not need to say anything further.

E: You have told quite a story, Philip. And I understand how Smith is gettiered in his belief that someone in the office owns a Corvette. Others in the office are gettiered on this proposition too I would presume. But I do not see how S is gettiered. According to the story, S knows that someone in the office owns a Corvette because his belief is grounded in the assumption that Jones owns a Corvette. S was gettiered before but he is not gettiered now.

P: Be patient, dear friend and listen to what happened next. Right after the security guard left the office, the other knowledge-workers and I began returning from lunch. As we exited the elevator, we saw Richard and Smith, who did not go with us to lunch, entering the office. We followed them in.

"Back from lunch so soon?" S asked.

"Smith and I never left," Richard answered. "We were hiding behind the potted plant in the hallway right outside the door this whole time. We heard your conversation with the security guard. So you think someone in the office is gettiered do you?"

S answered yes.

Smith then responded, "You think someone is gettiered because you think that I'm gettiered. But you are wrong S! I'm not gettiered—*I know*."

"You know what exactly? And how did you know I was thinking of you?" S replied. "And what do you mean when you say you are not gettiered? You think that someone in this office owns a Corvette because you think that Richard owns a Corvette. But Richard does not own a Corvette. It's a rental. And I can prove it."

"We know all about that S," Smith said. "We know you were here last night listening to Richard on the phone, we know you went into his cubicle, and we know you broke into his desk. In fact, we set the whole thing up."

"What?" S asked.

"That Corvette is mine," Richard explained. "The phone call you heard was fake. I knew you were in the office listening. There was nobody on the other end of the line. The billing invoices in my drawer? Also fake. The title on

---

8   H.P. Grice's paper, "Logic and Conversation," in *Syntax and Semantics*, Peter Cole and Jerry L. Morgan (eds.) (New York: Academic P, 1975) proposes various rules that govern conversation. The maxim of quantity says that speakers should make their contributions to the conversation as informative as required and no more.

the wall of my cubicle? It's not a fake car title. It's the real title doctored up to look like a fake. It's a fake fake title."

"Richard was not faking Corvette ownership," Smith explained. "He was faking the act of faking Corvette ownership.[9] And you fell for it. The whole thing was my idea. I've had my eye on you for a while now S. I could tell you were eaten up with jealousy over Richard's car. So we set you up. Big time."

"And you got burned more than once," Richard continued. "You thought I didn't own a Corvette and I do. And you thought Smith is gettiered in his belief that someone owns a Corvette but he isn't. He knows somebody who works here owns a Corvette because he knows I do. We take rides in it every weekend!"

"You are very clever," S conceded. "But here's something you don't know. I too know that someone in the office owns a Corvette. And I'm not talking about you, Richard."

"You think we don't know about that too?" Smith quickly snapped. "I live right next door to Jones. And guess what. He doesn't own a Corvette. Yes, there's a car in his garage that he inherited from his grandfather. But it's not a Corvette. It's a Chevette. He doesn't know the difference! Yeah, Jones is generally reliable. But you didn't seriously expect a tree hugger to know anything about cars did you? Have a blast tooling around in that Chevette this weekend."

"Look on the bright side," Richard added, "at least it's a step up from the Camry. Do you see what all your meddling has cost you S? If you had just minded your own business like everyone else around here and believed that I own a Corvette, you would have known that I own a Corvette and you would have known that someone in the office owns a Corvette. But you just had to go digging."

"The news of Jones's Chevette certainly depresses me," S responded. "And I'll also admit I was a little jealous of your car, Richard. But I take solace in knowing that my favorite pine tree transformed your treasured possession into a pile of fiberglass mulch. You must be deeply upset."

"I've got insurance," Richard replied. "And I never liked the reduced emissions package on those anyway. I think I'll swap her out for a '63 split window. But that's not your concern. What you ought to be thinking about is how your secret investigation only got you a bunch of second-order misleading evidence—evidence that made your other evidence look misleading when really it was the new evidence that was misleading. And because of that, you lost your

---

9   For more on the art and philosophy of the double fake see my "How to Fake Munchausen's Syndrome," *Philosophical Psychology* 23(5): 565–74 (2010).

knowledge that I own a Corvette and you lost your knowledge that someone in the office owns a Corvette."

"You're the worst kind of loser," Smith piled on, "a knowledge loser! But you couldn't stop there. You just had to go and gossip to Jones about it. And look what happened. You ended up getting a good reason to think that someone in the office owns a Corvette. And someone in the office does own a Corvette. But it's not Jones, it's Richard. First you knew, then you didn't. Then you went and gettiered yourself!"

"You're finished as a knowledge-worker, S," Richard announced. "Yeah, you got lots of attention back in the day. But it's over. You're all washed up. S *doesn't* know that P."

E: I hate to keep interrupting, Philip. And the story has certainly gotten more interesting with the addition of the second-order misleading evidence. But I remain rather disappointed. In one sense, what you have described is just another garden variety gettier case. S believes that someone in his office owns a Corvette because he believes that Jones owns a Corvette. And it is true that someone in the office owns a Corvette but it is not Jones, it is Richard. The road to this result twisted and turned but still, with all of his experience in the knowledge business, I would have expected much more out of S.

P: I still have not finished the story Ethan. I feel you are an overly eager lover of thought experiments. You must wait for the object of your passion to mature if you wish him to bear fruit.

E: You have my apologies, good sir. Proceed.

P: To everyone's surprise, S did not react in anger or outrage at Smith and Richard's words or at their manner of delivery. Instead, S sat in silence with his head tilted forward and his eyes nearly closed in deep contemplation. A hint of a smile formed upon his face as he lifted his head and began to speak.

And S spoke, "You are to be commended, Richard and Smith. It is one thing when knowledge-workers devise gettier cases from the desk chair but you have brought one to life. And it is one that raises very many questions.

"For instance, you assume that before my investigation last night, I knew that Richard owns a Corvette. I suppose you also think everyone else here, everyone who believed that Richard owns a Corvette, but didn't bother to inquire further—people like Philip for instance—these people all knew that Richard owns a Corvette. But anyone who took a careful look at the title on your wall would have also been suspicious about your Corvette. So it is only through a kind of carelessness, a failure to consider the evidence that was right in front of him, that Philip and the others did not also begin to suspect that you did not own that Corvette. But why should they have knowledge when I did not? Why should Philip's carelessness give him an epistemic advantage? Why should a failure of diligence—which, like all epistemic failures, is at bottom a kind of stupidity—ever enable one to know *more*?[10]

"Then I wonder about our security guard. I told him that someone in the office was gettiered in his belief that someone in the office owns a Corvette. I said that because I had very good reason to believe that Smith had been gettiered in his belief that someone in this office owns a Corvette. At that time, Smith was not gettiered in that belief. But I was. Therefore, when I told the security guard that someone in the office was gettiered in his belief that someone in this office owns a Corvette, I said something true but it was not something I knew.

"Now we must ask: Did the security guard gain knowledge from my testimony? We might think one can know that P via someone else's testimony only if the testifier knows that P.[11] If that is correct, then the security guard did not know that someone in this office is gettiered in his belief that someone in this office owns a Corvette. And, since this was his basis for thinking that someone in the office owns a Corvette, he did not know that either. But it really didn't matter. The security guard went on his way and, presumably, has now determined that Richard owns the car that was destroyed. So why does it matter whether we actually know? On the other hand, we might think testimonial knowledge does not require the testifier to know that P. And one might see our security guard as a point in favor of that idea.

"These, however, are all minor concerns compared to what I have to say now. Over the years, some of you have seen me carving slash marks on the front of my desk and wondered why I do that. I carve a mark into my desk whenever a knowledge-worker is gettiered. And, as the marks show, it happens more than you think. This is why I always carry my penknife. You'll also notice the mark on the far right is fresh. I put it there this morning. As we know, I believed, with very good reason, that Smith was gettiered. And from that I inferred, quite naturally, that someone in the office is gettiered. Hence, the final fresh mark."

E: Ah ha, Philip! I finally see!

P: You do?

> Would we expect someone who is gettiered in his belief that this is the way to Larissa will get there just as well as one who knows? If not, is this because the gettiered person lacks knowledge or because the gettiered person also possesses a false belief?

---

10 For a further exploration of this question, see Catherine Elgin's "The Epistemic Efficacy of Stupidity," *Synthese* 74(3): 297–311 (1988).
11 This is what Jennifer Lackey calls the "transmission thesis." For a discussion and critique, see her book *Learning from Words* (Oxford: Oxford UP, 2008).

E: Yes. S believes that someone in the office is gettiered. And that belief is itself a gettiered belief! When he carved that mark into his desk, S had a justified true belief that someone in the office is gettiered but he did not know that someone in the office is gettiered because it wasn't the person S thought—it was not Smith who was gettiered—it was S himself. *S got gettiered at the very instant he believed that someone is gettiered.* His belief that someone is gettiered is itself yet another gettier and, I think I can say, the finest gettier of them all.

P: Indeed. S's deduction is what we might call a self-fulfilling gettier inference—his conclusion that someone is gettiered, because it is based on a false but justified assumption, *makes itself true.*

Many of the other knowledge-workers, including me, had by this time gathered around S's cubicle. As you can imagine, some of the knowledge-workers were creating quite a disturbance upon hearing what S had just said. Like you, we realized that S got gettiered at the very moment he believed that someone was gettiered. But we had not yet begun to appreciate the implications of this.

"Knowledge-workers, please!" S spoke over the uproarious crowd. "Calm yourselves for a moment. If you do not cease your shouting, I will have the security guard come back and remove you from the building. Reflect upon the epistemic properties of my belief that someone in the office is gettiered. In addition to its self-fulfilling character, this belief, as you see, exhibits all the hallmarks of a classic gettier case. It is a justified true belief essentially based upon a false assumption. But, on the other hand, my belief that someone is gettiered also possesses the very properties some say distinguish knowledge from mere true opinion.

"Consider the well-known property of 'safety.' A belief is safe when it could not have easily been false.[12] My belief that someone in the office is gettiered possesses this cherished epistemic property. I formed my belief that someone in the office is gettiered only after a careful consideration of the evidence. And, in spite of my evidence, Smith had not been gettiered. But, since Smith was not gettiered, someone else in the office was, namely, me. Given the circumstances, my inference from my belief that Smith is gettiered to my conclusion that someone in this office is gettiered was, in a certain way, immune to error. If the premise is true, then that premise makes the conclusion true. If the premise is false, then the fact that I made the inference and had good evidence for the conclusion makes the conclusion true. Given the manner in which I formed my belief that someone is gettiered, it could hardly have turned out that *no one* was gettiered. It is certainly a safe belief.

---

12 This sort of position is discussed in Chapter 2: Barney and Arnie Take a Ride.

"Consider also the well-known and related 'sensitivity' condition on knowledge. Some say what distinguishes knowledge that P from mere true belief that P is that the subject would not have believed that P if P were false.[13] A moment's reflection reveals that my belief that someone in the office is gettiered meets this condition. If it were false that someone in the office is gettiered, in other words, if no one here is gettiered, I would not have believed that someone in the office is gettiered because I got gettiered by forming the belief that someone is gettiered. Were I not gettiered, I would not have believed that someone was.

"My belief that someone in the office is gettiered exhibits the definitive traits of knowledge, at least according to some accounts. But my belief that someone in the office is gettiered is itself a classic case of a gettiered belief. It is a justified true belief based upon a false assumption. And let us not forget, my fellow knowledge-workers, that safety and sensitivity have both been said to explain why gettiered subjects *do not* know. Does this not mean that one can be gettiered and yet still know that P? Or must we now say that I both know and do not know that someone in the office is gettiered?"

Upon hearing this, the knowledge-workers could no longer contain themselves.

E: I can certainly see why.

P: Smith and Richard and some of the other Richards that had gathered there burst forth with shouts and cries.

"Nonsense!" Smith shouted first and loudest as was his wont. "It has been proven that one can have knowledge from false assumptions.[14] This only shows that you don't understand what it is to be gettiered!"

E: That is a very serious accusation.

P: Indeed it is. But not all of the shouting and screaming was born of hostility. One of the other Richards called out, "Of course you cannot be gettiered and know that P! This is yet another reason to reject safety and sensitivity accounts of knowledge. Hooray for S!"

Others shouted things too but, by this time, there was so much commotion among the crowd it was difficult to make out who was saying what. I heard someone yelling that "counterfactuals depend on context" and they are

---

13 The idea that knowledge is sensitive true belief is developed and defended by Robert Nozick in *Philosophical Explanations* (Cambridge: Cambridge UP, 1981). Nozick's view is a close cousin of Dretske's idea that knowledge is true belief based upon a "conclusive reason."
14 For an argument to this effect see Ted Warfield's "Knowledge from Falsehood," *Philosophical Perspectives* 5: 405–15 (2005). For an alternative point of view see my "Knowledge with and without Belief," *Metaphilosophy* 45(1): 120–32 (2014).

"difficult to assess" and someone kept shouting about "backtracking" but it was impossible to discern any more than this amongst all the noise. Near the rear of the crowd, there appeared to be pushing and shoving and elbowing taking place among a few of the other Richards.

E: My heavens.

P: But S remained unperturbed. He sat in his desk chair with his arms folded and waited until things settled down. The he addressed the crowd a final time.

"Of course I am aware that there are those who think one can have knowledge based upon false assumptions," S began. "But I am more interested in the remark from one of the other Richards that this situation only presents a problem for safety and sensitivity views.

"I neglected to mention that while I was carving that last mark into my desk, I reflected upon my reason for thinking that someone in the office is gettiered. I was well aware that, being empirically grounded, my belief that Smith is gettiered isn't absolutely certain. But I was also aware of the massive amount of evidence I had for thinking that Smith is gettiered. I was aware that I was justified in believing that Smith is gettiered. And then the self-fulfilling character of my inference became apparent. It dawned on me that if, in spite of all my evidence, Smith isn't gettiered, then, in virtue of my believing that someone in the office is gettiered, *I* am thereby gettiered. Specifically, I am gettiered in my belief that someone in the office is gettiered. Further reflection thus brought forth in my mind the following line of argument:

1. Either Smith is gettiered or not.
2. If Smith is gettiered then someone in the office is gettiered.
3. If Smith is not gettiered, then my belief that someone in the office is gettiered is essentially grounded on a justified but false assumption, in which case, someone in the office is gettiered (namely, me).

----

4. So either way, someone in the office is gettiered.

The premises here are true and the inference is valid. Yet the conclusion is true only because I was gettiered. The paradox therefore is not limited to safety and sensitivity views. Under any view of knowledge that requires the knower to be aware of his reasons, and of course under the no false lemmas view of knowledge,[15] my belief is both gettiered and known. Or, what amounts to the same thing, both known and not known."

---

15 This view was first proposed by Michael Clark, "Knowledge and Grounds: A Comment on Mr. Gettier's Paper," *Analysis* 24: 46–48 (1963). It says knowledge is a justified true belief not

E: The other knowledge-workers must have erupted after such an offensive remark!

P: To my surprise they did not. It is as if S's speech had sapped all their energy. There was no more shouting or screaming or shoving. But one of the other Richards lowly grumbled that there is no paradox because S has two belief tokens with the same content. One of them is knowledge and one of them is not.

E: That is a very curious remark.

P: And one I shall not attempt to decipher. Then Smith muttered, as if only to himself, that the problem would not exist if S had been careful enough to time-index his different beliefs. He raised his voice slightly and said, "Gettiered *at t*."

> Does this or one of the other Richards's remark provide the basis for a solution to S's paradox?

E: Perhaps he too was concerned with those blue and green emeralds.

P: I do not know and there would have been no point in asking as that was all anyone had left. The crowd fell silent.

It was then that S unfolded his arms and lifted himself up from his desk chair without saying anything and stood there before the crestfallen knowledge-workers. S stretched and straightened his legs as he stood because his legs had become heavy from being seated at his desk for so long. The crowd dispersed and the knowledge-workers lumbered back to their cubicles. And S began walking—unsteadily because his legs were still stiff and heavy—toward the exit. On his way, he passed Greco's cubicle.

"Oh, Greco," S said as he left the office for the day, "we owe Edmund a Coke. Buy him one and do not forget."[16]

This, Ethan, is how our friend S got gettiered, this knowledge-worker who, we would say, is the most justified and true and undefeated anyone has ever known.

---

based upon any false assumptions. The idea has been recently defended by Lycan in "On the Gettier Problem Problem." Richard Feldman's *Epistemology* expresses sympathy for it as well.
16 Among knowledge-workers, it is traditional to sacrifice a Coke to Edmund—the god of modern epistemology—whenever one gets gettiered.

The Philosophy of Philosophical Writing Revisited
Departmental Meeting

The following is transcribed from a tape of a meeting of the senior faculty of the philosophy department. To preserve confidentiality, names of committee members have been redacted. Due to severe budget cuts, the meeting was recorded using very poor equipment over what appears to be an old tape of various philosophy department guest lectures. As a result, certain portions of the meeting are missing and material from the old recordings comes through. These technical difficulties are noted in the transcript.

Committee Member 1: Where's [name redacted]?

Committee Member 2: He teaches online.

Committee Member 3: So he doesn't have to come to meetings?

M1: Guess I should start teaching online.

M2: You've certainly got the face for teaching online.

Chairperson: We have a quorum. You all know why we're here. Who'd like to begin?

M3: I will. I have a problem with this guy's publication record. There's a couple piddling little journal articles—low-tier stuff—and then there's this book of dialogues. Did you read this thing? What kind of philosophy book is this? It's full of jokes! I don't think this guy takes philosophy seriously.

M2: Judging by the jokes, I'd say he doesn't take comedy too seriously either.

M3: Yeah. An Arnold Schwarzenegger impression? Total hackwork.

M1: Hold on. Just because somebody's having fun, that doesn't mean he's not taking philosophy seriously. Wittgenstein once said he wanted to write a philosophy book that consisted of nothing but jokes.

M2: He wrote it.

M1: He did?

M2: Yeah, it's called *Tractatus Logico-Philosophicus*.

M3: Now that is a joke.

M1: What he said or the *Tractatus*?

M3: True.

M2: Inclusive.

M3: Even aside from all the crappy jokes, I have a problem with the format of the thing. I mean, nobody writes dialogues anymore! And with good reason.

M1: What's the reason?

M3: Dialogues are not real philosophy.

M2: Yeah, just look at it. There are no conclusions. It's all pointless.

M1: I disagree. Take the chapter with the brains in vats for example.

M2: What about it?

M1: Famous solutions to the problem of skepticism are presented and critiqued. But it is all done by brains in vats trying to use these anti-skeptical epistemologies to prove that they know they *don't* have hands. And the "skeptic" is somebody who thinks maybe they have hands after all.

M2: I got that part. Real cute. But what's the point?

M3: I was wondering the same thing. I get that some of the usual arguments have been flipped. That's a nice exercise. But I don't see anything new or interesting. If anything, the flipping device just obfuscates things.

M1: I disagree. I think there is a very important point being made here. As I see it, the point is that all of these solutions—

meeting recording interrupted

Unidentified Guest Speaker 1: AAAAAnnnnd Uhhhh Sssso Uhh forrrrr FRAYYYguh! thee REFrence! of theee uhhh NAYYYYM! is uhhHHHHHH—

meeting recording resumes

M1: —recasts the debate.

M3: I hadn't thought of it like that.

M2: But why not just say all that in a paper? Why hide behind the dialogue form and a bunch of lame jokes? Unless you are just trying to get out of defending what you say.

M1: Filmmakers will often put short comedic scenes in the middle of serious dramatic movies to give the audience a chance to come up for air and digest things. In the typical philosophy paper, nothing like that ever happens. That's part of what makes them all so unreadable. But only part. I think Wittgenstein can help us here too.

M2: Speaking of unreadable.

M1: Remember the distinction between saying and showing? Perhaps the philosophical dialogue is more the latter.

M3: But if you can say it why show it?

M2: Or whistle it.

M3: Exactly. Any point you can make in a dialogue, you can make in a regular paper or book. There's no philosophical payoff to this form. That's why it's been dead for so long. Good riddance.

M1: Here's an important difference. In an ordinary philosophy book, the ideal is to spoon-feed the reader your arguments and conclusions so clearly and so persuasively that The Truth will be passively absorbed right off the page and into the brain. The dialogue doesn't aspire to that. It asks more of the reader. And maybe there's some value in figuring things out yourself. Isn't figuring it out yourself an essential part of the philosophical process? Isn't that what philosophy teachers tell their students?

M2: I never do. If they were capable of figuring things out, they wouldn't need me.

M3: Yeah, people today want answers and philosophers should be giving them what they want. Not a bunch of questions and disagreements.

M1: I think there might also be a philosophical reason behind choosing the dialogue form especially if you're the kind of philosopher who is sympathetic to skeptical views. If that's where you're coming from, it would be a bit disingenuous, maybe even self-contradictory, to write in the didactic fashion of the typical philosophy paper or book—as if you're proving something. So perhaps the entire book is supposed to serve as some sort of implicit critique of the traditional pretensions of philosophical writing. I've always thought something like that helps explain why Nietzsche wrote the way he did.

M2: What a load of crap.

M3: Yeah, a load of crap he can neither carry nor cast off.

M2: And when you look into this crap, it looks also into you.

M1: But maybe it would be a good idea to address some of these meta-philosophical questions in an appendix. That could even be done in dialogue form.

M3: Just what we need. More of this guy's dialogues. Look, if you've got a beef with how philosophy is usually done, say so and make your case. Like I said, anything you can do in a dialogue you can do in a regular paper.

M1: Why does the dialogue have to do something the ordinary philosophy paper can't do? If a dialogue can do what other sorts of philosophical writing can and the others have value then the dialogue does too. With any kind of philosophical work, if you read it with the intent of finding something to complain about, you will succeed. Maybe it's easier to do that with a dialogue. But maybe that's a strike against the reader rather than the book.

M3: But if you're a philosopher—a *real* philosopher—and you're reading a work of philosophy, it's your job to find something to complain about. Everything you are saying in defense of this book could be said in defense of any terrible book in pseudo-philosophy or new age metaphysics. "Oh, it's an implicit critique of the traditional methods," "It asks more of the reader," "Showing versus saying." All lame. If we allow this crank to pass, who're we gonna end with up next? L. Ron Hu—

meeting recording interrupted

Unidentified Speaker 2: [*in British, possibly Australian*] —with the caveat that I didn't get around to writing a paper or reading anything on this topic. But I thought about the issue some on the tram from the airport this morning. So I have a great deal to say that you will want to hear. I shall try to stay on shedual and begin by distinguishing—

meeting recording resumes

M3: —about the chapter on pragmatic encroachment? This is supposed to be a case where knowledge ebbs and flows as the stakes go up and down. I get that. But he never considers the idea that an error possibility might remain salient even after the stakes have shifted from high to low. So the pragmatic encroachment thesis doesn't commit you to thinking you should reverse your epistemic judgments as the stakes shift. Furthermore, proponents of the pragmatic encroachment thesis already admit that when we occupy high stakes situations we tend to deny knowledge claims concerning our counterparts in corresponding low stakes situations. But there are several explanations for this. First, we project our own situation onto others.[1] Second, we confuse the question "Does S know that P?" with "If S were in my situation, would S know that P?"[2]

M1: But you mustn't forget that this is a case where the subject is herself a philosopher and a proponent of the pragmatic encroachment thesis. There's no reason why such a person would commit the elementary mistakes of projecting her own situation on somebody else or confusing those two questions. For the same reason, I can't see why an error possibility would remain salient for a person if that person is aware that only the stakes have shifted and the stakes are irrelevant to the truth of the proposition under consideration. And if you think something called "salience" guides epistemic judgments independent of stakes, it seems you've shifted away from the pragmatic encroachment view and to something more like a contextualis—

Committee Member 4: I hate to interrupt, but you three have had the floor for the entire meeting. And there's something that's been bothering me the whole time about this book. It concerns the chapter you are discussing. This chapter describes vicious criminal activity including a brutal murder. At the very least, the book needs to include a trigger warn—

meeting recording interrupted

9 minutes of unintelligible mumbling followed by 42 seconds of enthusiastic applause

meeting recording resumes

---

1 John Hawthorne offers this hypothesis in *Knowledge and Lotteries* (Oxford: Oxford UP, 2003), 162–66.
2 Jason Stanley offers this hypothesis in *Knowledge and Practical Interests* (Oxford: Oxford UP, 2005), 101.

M3: —department needs people who do *real philosophy*. And that means more than just rehearsing the same tired old arguments and objections even if you do it in a cutesy way. I mean, look at this chapter on the preface paradox. Sure, it's neat to wonder about how someone who thinks it's irrational to believe that everything in your book is true would approach a courtroom oath. But beyond that there's nothing new here. It's just the same old arguments applied in a new context peppered over with more terrible jokes.

M1: I disagree. The chapter contains several fresh criticisms of what has arguably become the orthodox position on this important epistemic paradox. I see this chapter as extending the preceding chapter's criticisms of closure—

meeting recording interrupted

Unidentified Speaker 4: Can you see it now?

Audience Member 1: It's out of focus!

Audience Member 2: It's too small!

US4: Gosh I don't know how to—

Audience Member 3: Maybe if you just moved the projector back some it would—

US4: Oh, the projector stand is on wheels. Good. I'll just push the whole thing back and—oh no, the cord came out. Is there an extension cord somewhere?

AM1: Steven, will you run back to the office and get the extension cord?

38 minutes of uninterrupted silence, presumably while audience waits for Steven to find extension cord

meeting recording resumes

M2: —diculous conversation with a robot who eats sushi.

Chairperson: It sounds like we keep returning to the same points. I'm going to have to cut things off here because I have an important meeting with the Dean at 3:30. As most of you know, I was selected to serve on the committee to select the Search Committee to select our new Assistant Chair of the Acting Associate Vice Provost's Leadership Excellence Assessment Oversight for Regional and Global Wellness Advancement Outreach Awareness Council. So I really can't stay here to discuss this small matter much longer.

M3: The CSSAC LEAORGWAOAC? That's an important one. Better wrap this up.

M4: And my son needs a ride home from school. I move that we call the question.

M3: I second.

M2: The motion or needing a ride from school?

C: All those in favor s—

tape ends

Appendix on the Purpose and Limits of Philosophical Inquiry
Cartesian Auto

You want to take a long road trip so you dropped your car off at a shop around the corner to have it checked out. You call in the afternoon to see how things went.

Ring

R: Cartesian Car Care. A stable and lasting foundation for all your automotive needs.

Y: Hello Rene. I dropped my Daewoo off earlier today to have it checked out for my road trip?

R: Oh yeah. They're finishing up right now. Everything seems fine.

Y: Okay great. I'll pick it up. LA here I come.

R: Ah, well we can't let you have her just yet. We checked the car but we still need to check the methods we used to do that.

Y: The methods?

R: Yeah. You see, in the process of checking your car, we relied on various sophisticated instruments and gauges and whatnot.

Y: You're worried your instruments are busted?

R: They could be. These things aren't infallible. Any shop that says otherwise is full of it. Gauges and instruments can fail. Everybody knows that.

Y: How long will that take?

R: It's a little more complicated than that.

Y: How so?

R: We check the instruments and gauges and against other instruments and gauges. But how do we know the others aren't also busted? There are other methods at work here too: induction, abduction. We'll need to do a full methodological evaluation before we can hand this thing over.

Y: You'll have to slow down a bit. I'm not familiar with all these automotive terms.

R: Epistemological terms. You see, induction is a process of reasoning that allows us to infer things about the future based on how they've been the past. For example, you believe the shad will start running in the spring—

Y: The what?

R: The shad. You fish don't you?

Y: No.

R: Doesn't matter. You believe they'll run in the spring because that's the way it's been every year for as long as anybody can remember. Or you would if you fished.

Y: I see. So what's the problem?

R: How do you know the future will turn out like the past? How do we know induction is a reliable process of reasoning? Turns out the only justification we can give for thinking induction will work is that it has in the past. But that's just more induction! And that's circular reasoning. I can't send you out on the highway with nothing but a circular argument. People could die.

Y: Uh-huh.

R: And abduction's got some serious problems too once you look under the hood.

Y: Ab what?

R: Abduction. You know, inference to the best explanation. Very useful to us mechanics. Like when one of my guys hears your catalytic converter clinking and clanking? He concludes it's a loose piece of ceramic rattling around. He didn't *see* a loose piece of ceramic but it's the best explanation for what he saw.

Y: Heard.

R: Exactly. Now here's the thing: what makes an explanation the best? People talk about simplicity and stuff like that but why think the simpler hypothesis

APPENDIX ON THE PURPOSE AND LIMITS OF PHILOSOPHICAL INQUIRY

is more likely to be true? And how do you know that the correct explanation is among the group of explanations you're considering? I mean, if you consider all the possible hypotheses that would explain any particular set of phenomena, there's gonna be a whole bunch of 'em—darn near infinite in fact. So chances are the one you landed on will be incorrect. You've got a major bad lot problem here we'll need to look into.[1]

Y: Bad lot? Sounds serious.

R: I hate to tell you but there's more. Observation based on sense perception was fundamental to the entire process of checking out your car. But why think observation is a reliable guide to the way the world is?

Y: You think you need your eyes checked?

R: There's that. But beyond that, we also need to figure out whether anybody's observations can be trusted ever. I mean, I think I checked your car and it looks fine but how do I know I wasn't just dreaming that? How do I know I'm not dreaming right now? We're gonna need to run a full EDD on this puppy.

Y: EDD?

R: Evil Demon Diagnostic. You might have evil demons in your cooling system, your steering box. Hell, you can even have an evil demon hiding in the cigarette lighter.

Y: Do cars still have those?

R: Oh yeah. Even with all this new technology, modern cars aren't demon proof.

Y: I was talking about cigarette lighters.

R: Thing is, if there was an evil demon, everything'd look just fine. That's the problem with those damn things. And that's why we gotta run the EDD.

Y: Sounds expensive.

R: Expensive? Look, my granddaddy founded this business and he taught me that an evil demon can deceive you even about basic truths of arithmetic. So I can't total up your bill unless I know I've arrived at the right sum. And I can't do that until I know there's not an evil demon in your car messing up my math. You wanna talk expensive? How would you feel if I overcharged you? Then you'd've paid too much *and* you'd still have a demon!

---

1 For more on the bad lot and other objections to inference to the best explanation see Bas van Fraassen, *Laws and Symmetry* (New York: Oxford UP, 1989), 146.

Y: But if evil demons are so powerful, won't they be able to trick the EDD device?

R: You're starting to see how serious the problem is here buddy.

Y: I appreciate you looking out for me like this. But it sounds like some of these questions you're asking are inappropriate.

R: Oh, you wanna talk inappropriate? You should get a look at this calendar the Snap-On guy dropped off the other day.

Y: Not that kind of inappropriate. I'm saying: Do we really need to worry about dreams and evil demons? I'm just trying to get to LA.

R: So you think maybe we shouldn't even be asking these questions. Way ahead of you. That's another thing we've gotta figure out here. We've gotta check out your car, check the methods we used, check the methods for checking those methods, and we've gotta figure out whether it's legitimate to check into these things in the first place. Here at Cartesian, we pride ourselves on providing full service auto care—right down to the fundamentals. And this means we're willing to consider *any* problem that concerns your car. Including the evil demon problem. And the problem of whether we really oughta be worrying about problems like that. This is why we're the best and most thorough auto repair service you can find. Now my parts guy, Chuck—you know, down at Peirce Parts? He's got no time for evil demons and all that. He thinks those are just "paper doubts."[2] And maybe he's right. But how do we sort the paper from the metal? And is he saying I *know* I'm not dreaming? How could I know that? But you can't expect a parts guy to know too much about cars.

Y: You know, this is all fascinating but I think I'll just come down and—

R: Whoa! Sorry to interrupt you there buddy but one of my guys just handed me a note. He went ahead and swapped out your serpentine belt. It was showing some serious signs of wear.

Y: Oh, okay. Thanks.

R: Don't thank me yet. Here's the thing: he thinks he may have destroyed your car in the process.

Y: Destroyed my car! What happened?

---

2 In "The Fixation of Belief," *Popular Science Monthly* 12(1): 1–15 (1877), C.S. Peirce complains that the radically skeptical doubts one finds in philosophers like Descartes are not genuine but merely "set down upon paper."

R: Well, you see, since the parts are now different it might be that the car you brought in has ceased to exist.

Y: How can a car cease to exist just by changing one of its parts?

R: Maybe it can't. Maybe anytime you have a car and you change one of its parts, it keeps its identity. But then it looks like if we swapped your car's parts one by one, we'd still have the same car at the end of the process.

Y: Sounds fine to me.

R: Wait'll you see the bill. Now suppose each time we removed an old part, we stuck it in a pile. And then from the pile of old parts we built a whole 'nother car. Which one's yours? And why?

Y: Alright. Look, I think I'll just come and get my car and—

R: You aren't listening. How can I give you *your car* if I don't know whether it exists? I can't just hand over any old car and say it's yours. This is a reputable business were running here.

Y: I didn't mean to insult you I just want my—er, I mean a car or—

R: I'd feel terrible if we destroyed your car buddy. And, of course, you'd need to talk to my insurance guy about getting it replaced. I was worried about the epistemology. But now it looks like you've got metaphysical issues here too. Those always show up once you get a lotta miles and have to start replacing parts. Heck, sometimes metaphysical problems show up on a car right out of the factory.

Y: Wouldn't that be covered under manufacturer's warranty?

R: Manufacturers cover the parts but not the metaphysics. Nobody wants anything to do with metaphysics anymore. Not even the Germans. But they used to. Oh boy, did they ever. These days, people'll throw parts at you all day long. But nobody bothers to look at the metaphysics and ask whether that's even the same car. In fact, we're the only shop in the Carolinas that knows how to work on that stuff. You're really lucky you came in when you did.

Y: I don't feel so lucky.

R: Oh yeah?

Y: Yeah. I mean, like I said, I appreciate your hard work and all but I can't help but think that if I had gone to another mechanic I wouldn't be spending all this money on labor for a bunch of philosophical problems. And I'd already be on my way to LA. I don't see why we've got to ask all these questions about epistemology and metaphysics just to fix a car.

R: Tell you what. There's an acupuncture clinic down the street. Why don't I just drop your Daewoo off there? Or, better yet, there's a church up the road where they got a blind guy does faith healing with an albino rattlesnake. Why not have him fix you up?

Y: Huh?

R: Yeah, I know what you're thinking. Acupuncture? Faith healing? Snakes? Well those ain't good methods for working on cars!

Y: Right. But I was also thinking about the paint job.

R: Absolutely. Don't let 'em get them needles anywhere near your rustproofing. Now look, you aren't gonna let a faith healer work on your car because you've got no good reason to think that faith healing works. But what good reason do you have to think induction works? That it has in the past? Well, gee buddy, the snake handler down the street says he knows God speaks to him because God told him so last time they talked. How's that any worse?

Y: What's that guy's address again?

R: We realize that people think the kinds of questions we're asking are stupid or "inappropriate" or whatever. But you know what? We'll stop asking 'em when somebody gives a good answer. And nobody has.

Y: Well yeah but usually these questions don't arise in an auto shop. That way, people can just get on with fixing cars.

R: Don't arise? What do you mean "don't arise"? Look, just because nobody's asking these questions doesn't mean they aren't there. That's like saying that since the guy didn't look for a leak on your rear diff, there isn't one because the question "didn't arise." Or it's like saying there's no issue about whether faith healing really works because the people who believe in it never bother to ask. Every auto mechanic has all these same questions; they're just too lazy to confront them. But we aren't like that. We're serious. It's not that we're doing something wrong by caring about these questions, it's that everybody else is for not. Like I said, FULL SERVICE AUTO CARE.

Y: I get that in order to determine what's wrong my car, you need to run some sort of test. And, whatever test you use, it will need to be a good one. But you seem to think that's not enough. You also have to *know* that the test you used to determine what's wrong with my car is a good one. But then you'll need to run another test. A test to test the test.

R: A test to test the test? Nice. I realize you don't know jack about cars buddy. But I think you might have a mechanic's soul. You should check out our apprentice program. We're always looking for people.

Y: My point is it never ends. Even if you do a test to test the test, you can't stop there. What good is the test you used to test the test if that test is untested? So you'll need to run another test to test the test you used for testing the test. And the test that tests the test that tested the test will need to be tested by another test. This is insane!

R: Don't get testy with me, buddy.

Y: If you're such a careful mechanic, why don't you think about this? If you want to know what's wrong with the car, maybe it's enough to run a good reliable test. Maybe you don't need to know that the test is a good one. Ever think of that?

R: Did we ever think of that? Remember who you're dealing with here pal. Our shop has a board certified infinite regress specialist. Lots of places subcontract that work out. Not us. And sure, you can say a good test is all you need; you don't need to test the test and you don't need to know that the test is good. But, if you don't know whether your test is a good one, there is an element of faith involved in the whole process. And then what do you say to the snake priest? Why not just let him work on your ride? And lemme point out another thing here, buddy. The whole question of whether it's ever okay to ignore hard philosophical questions is itself a hard philosophical question. So any shop that says they can just "set aside" philosophy is already doing philosophy. And that means they're contradicting themselves. Is that where you want to take your car buddy? To a mechanic who goes around contradicting himself?

Y: I'm tempted. But now you're telling me you don't even know if my car still exists and even if it does you might need to run an infinite number of tests before you can say it's safe to drive.

R: Sounds like you're finally getting it. I thought you'd never come around. Meantime, how 'bout we hook you up with a loaner?

Y: You have loaners?

R: Lots. We have to.

Y: I'll bet.

R: Citroen okay? It's French.

call dropped

Acknowledgments

An earlier version of Chapter 5 was published under the title "What's It Like to Be a BIV? A Dialogue," in the *Journal of the American Philosophical Association* 1(4): 734–56 (2015).

I thank Stephen Latta and Bob Martin of Broadview Press along with several anonymous reviewers for helpful comments on earlier versions of this book. This book also benefitted from discussion with George Bailey, Gerry Beaulieu, John Collins, Ed Erwin, Nick Georgalis, A.J. Kreider, Jeremy Morris, Jay Newhard, Len Olsen, and Frank Winberry.

Index

abominable conjunctions, 28–29
"The Argument from Abomination," 33n10
Austin, J.L.
    "Other Minds," 88n32
    Sense and Sensibilia, 71n6, 83n22

Beebe, James, "The Abductivist Reply to Skepticism," 73n10
Berkeley, George, 70, 98
Bisson, Terry, "They're Made Out of Meat," 128n12
BonJour, Laurence, "The Indispensability of Internalism," 70n2
Borges, Luis, *Labyrinths*, 98n47
Bouwsma, O.K., "Descartes' Evil Genius," 82n19
brains in vats, 69–71, 73
Brueckner, Anthony
    "Brains in a Vat," 91n36
    "Contextualism, SSI and the Factivity Problem," 108n3
Buford, Christopher, 108n3
bullshit, 75

Carroll, Lewis, "What the Tortoise Said to Achilles," 31n7
Charniak, Christopher, *Minimal Rationality*, 77n12
Chinese Room, 124n8, 125–26, 126n9, 127, 133

Christensen, David
    "Disagreement, Question-Begging and Epistemic Self-Criticism," 130n13
    "The Epistemology of Controversy," 142n22
    "The Epistemology of Disagreement," 119n1
circularity objection, 70
Clark, Michael, "Knowledge and Grounds," 160n15
closure-denial, 25, 28, 62
closure-principle, 28n2
Cole, David, "The Chinese Room Argument," 125n8
Collins, John
    "Epistemic Closure Principles," 25n1
    "The Evil God Challenge," 98n45
commonsense, 8, 73, 79, 83
commonsense worldview, 87
conciliatory view of disagreement, 120–21, 132, 137, 139–40, 142, 145
conclusive reasons, 34, 159n13
consciousness, 125, 127–28
contextualism, 72, 88
contextualist theories, 108n3

Davidson, Donald
    "A Coherence Theory of Truth and Knowledge," 92n38
    "The Method of Truth in Metaphysics," 92n37
deductive closure, 25
defeaters (rebutting or undermining), 55–56, 59
DeRose, Keith, 28
    The Case for Contextualism, 72n9
    "Contextualism and Knowledge Attributions," 100n2
    "Solving the Skeptical Problem," 28n3, 89n33, 90n34
Descartes, René, 9, 174n2
different evidence, 83
disagreement, 119, 129–30, 133
    conciliatory view of, 120–21, 132, 137, 139–40, 142, 145
    steadfast views of, 120–21
disagreement about the direction of defeat, 59
disagreements between epistemic peers. *See* peer disagreement
double fake, 155n9
Dretske, Fred, 25–28, 61, 159n13
    "The Case against Closure," 25n1, 31n6, 32n8, 33n9
    "Conclusive Reasons," 37n13
    "Epistemic Operators," 29n4
    "Reply to Hawthorne," 39n14, 41n16

Elgin, Catherine, "The Epistemic Efficacy of Stupidity," 157n10
environmental epistemology, 8, 11
Epictetus, *The Enchiridion*, 96n44
epistemic closure principles, 25n1
epistemic value, 22–23
ethical egoism, 138
externalist interpretation of conciliatory view of disagreement, 140

factivity problem, 108n3
Feldman, Richard
    Epistemology, 147, 148n2, 160n15
    "Respecting the Evidence," 120n3
Frankfurt, Harry, *On Bullshit*, 75n11
Fumerton, Richard, "Skepticism and Naturalistic Epistemology," 20n14

Gettier, Edmund, 8
    "Is Justified True Belief Knowledge?," 59n9, 147n1
Goldman, Alan, 43–45
    "A Note on the Conjunctivity of Knowledge," 44n2
Goldman, Alvin, 8n2
    "Discrimination and Perceptual Knowledge," 7n1
    "What Is Justified Belief?," 12n8, 69n1, 79n14
Goldman's Variation on the Preface, 51
Goldstein, Laurence, *Clear and Queer Thinking*, 36n12
Goodman, Nelson, *Fact, Fiction and Forecast*, 150n6
Grice, H.P., "Logic and Conversation," 154n8
Grundman, Thomas, "Doubts about Philosophy?," 120n4

Haddock, Adrian, *Epistemic Value*, 23n20
Hawthorne, John
    "Knowledge and Action," 112n5
    Knowledge and Lotteries, 45n3, 167n1
heap paradox. *See* sorites paradox
Heidegger, Martin, *Being and Time*, 93n41
Hetherington, Stephen, "Knowing Failably," 147n1
Huemer, Michael, "Phenomenal Conservatism," 71n8
Hume, David, 58n8
    A Treatise on Human Understanding, 136n18
Hyde, Dominic, "Sorites Paradox," 45n4

idealism, 70, 98
independent evidence, 131

indistinguishability objection, 71
inference to the best explanation, 72, 94, 173n1
internalist conception of conciliatory view of disagreement, 140

James, William, *The Principles of Psychology*, 87n29
JTB theory of knowledge, 59, 147
justified true belief, 12n8, 160n15

Kant, Immanuel, 141
    Critique of Pure Reason, 93n40
Kelly, Thomas
    "Disagreement and Higher-Order Evidence," 141n21
    "The Epistemic Significance of Disagreement," 121n7
    "Evidence Can Be Permissive," 135n17
    "Historical *versus* Current Time Slice Theories in Epistemology," 134n15
Kim, Brian, "Surely This Paper Contains Some Errors?," 57n7
KK-thesis, 9
knowledge account of assertion, 17, 37
Kopec, Matthew, "The Uniqueness Thesis," 121n6
Kvanvig, Jonathan, *The Value of Knowledge and the Pursuit of Understanding*, 10n6

Lackey, Jennifer, *Learning from Words*, 157n11
Law, Stephen, "The Evil God Challenge," 97n45
Lewis, David
    "Counterfactual Dependence and Time's Arrow," 39n15
    "Veridical Hallucination and Prosthetic Vision," 87n31
Littlejohn, Clayton, "Disagreement and Defeat," 120n2
logical abomination, 33n10
Lycan, William, 148n4
    Judgment and Justification, 79n13, 85n26
    "Moore against the New Skeptics," 92n39
    "MPP, RIP," 31n5
    "On the Gettier Problem Problem," 8n3, 148n3, 160n15

Mankinson, David C., 43
    "The Paradox of the Preface," 43n1
Matheson, Jonathan, "Are Conciliatory Views of Disagreement Self-Defeating?," 120n5, 138n20
McGee, Vann, "A Counterexample to Modus Ponens," 31n5
Millar, Alan, 23n20

modus ponens, 31
Moore, G.E., 14, 70
    "Proof of an External World," 70n3, 80n15
Moore's paradox, 15, 32, 36
Moore's Paradox, 14n10
multi-premise closure denial, 60

Neo-Mooreanism, 70, 80
Nozik, Robert, 25
    Philosophical Explanations, 159n13

ontological argument, 141

paradox of material implication, 11, 14
Parfit, Derek, *Reasons and Persons*, 138n19
peer disagreement, 119–21, 133, 135, 137, 140–43, 145–46
Peirce, C.S.
    Collected Papers, 3n3
    "The Fixation of Belief," 174n2
perceptual knowledge, 27
Phenomenal Conservatism, 71
Plato
    "Crito," 117n6
    Meno, 9, 20n15, 21n17
Post, John, "Infinite Regresses of Justification and Explanation," 41n17
practical or instrumental value of knowledge, 22
pragmatic encroachment thesis, 100, 102, 108n3
preface paradox, 57n7
Principle of the Transitivity of Reasons, 41
Pritchard, Duncan, 23n20
    Epistemic Luck, 9n4
    Epistemological Disjunctivism, 81n18, 82n20, 84n24–25
    "Recent Work on Epistemic Value," 22n18
Pryor, James, "The Skeptic and the Dogmatist," 86n28, 87n30
Putnam, Hilary
    Realism with a Human Face, 2n2
    Reason, Truth and History, 91n35

Rabinowitz, Dani, "The Safety Condition on Knowledge," 9n4
rational response, 121, 130, 133
rebutting defeater, 55

reliabilism, 69–70, 79–80
right reasons view, 121, 133
Rosen, Gideon, "Nominalism, Naturalism, Epistemic Relativism," 121n6
Roth, Michael, "The Wall and the Shield," 148n4
Russell, Bertrand, 46n5, 126
    "The Analysis of Matter," 126n9
Ryle, Gilbert, 71
    The Concept of Mind, 71n4, 81n17

safety condition on knowledge, 9
Searle, John
    "Breaking the Hold," 128n11
    "Minds, Brains and Programs," 124n8
second-order knowledge, 17, 20
second-order skepticism, 9
Sextus Empiricus, *Outlines of Pyhhronism*, 145n23
simple reliabilism, 69, 79
skepticism, 8, 28, 69–70, 98
so what objection, 72
Sorensen, Roy
    "Dogmatism, Junk Knowledge and Conditionals," 14n9
    "Epistemic Paradoxes," 150n7
    Vagueness and Contradiction, 65n10, 66n11, 67n12
sorites paradox, 45, 64
Sosa, David, "Dubious Assertions," 15n12
S's paradox, 161
Stanley, Jason, 112n5
    Knowledge and Practical Interests, 99, 100n1, 109n4, 167n2
steadfast views of disagreement, 120–21
Steen, Mark, "Why Everyone Acts Altruistically All the Time," 98n46
Steup, Matthias, "In Defense of Internalism," 148n4
Stroud, Barry, "Understanding Human Knowledge in General," 70n2
swamping problem, 10, 23
Systems Reply to the Chinese Room argument, 126n9

Titelbaum, Michael, 121n6
"too iffy" objection, 70
traditional account of knowledge, 8
transmission thesis, 157n11
true belief, 12n8, 21–22, 160n15
Truth Connection Objection, 73

Tucker, Chris, "Why Open-Minded People Should Endorse Dogmatism," 86n27
Turing Test, 125–26, 134

uncertainty, 57
undermining defeater, 55
utilitarianism, 140

Van Frassen, Bas, *Laws and Symmetry*, 173n1
Veber, Michael
    "Contextualism and Semantic Ascent," 108n3
    "How to Fake Munchausen's Syndrome," 155n9
    "I Know I Am Not Gettiered," 149n4–5
    "Knowing What's Not Up the Road," 11n7
    "Knowledge with and without Belief," 159n14
Vogel, Jonathan, "Internalist Responses to Skepticism," 95n43

Warfield, Ted, "Knowledge from Falsehood," 159n14
Weiner, Matthew, "Norms of Assertion," 17n13
White, Roger, "Evidence Cannot Be Permissive," 135n16
Whitehead, A.N., *Process and Reality*, 2n1
Williamson, Timothy, 67n13
    Knowledge and Its Limits, 20n16, 71n5, 81n16
    "Scepticism and Evidence," 83n21, 83n23
    Vagueness, 65n10
Wittgenstein, Ludwig, *On Certainty*, 94n42

Zagzebski, Linda, "The Search for the Source of Epistemic Good," 22n19

From the Publisher

A name never says it all, but the word "Broadview" expresses a good deal of the philosophy behind our company. We are open to a broad range of academic approaches and political viewpoints. We pay attention to the broad impact book publishing and book printing has in the wider world; for some years now we have used 100% recycled paper for most titles. Our publishing program is internationally oriented and broad-ranging. Our individual titles often appeal to a broad readership too; many are of interest as much to general readers as to academics and students.

Founded in 1985, Broadview remains a fully independent company owned by its shareholders—not an imprint or subsidiary of a larger multinational.

For the most accurate information on our books (including information on pricing, editions, and formats) please visit our website at www.broadviewpress.com. Our print books and ebooks are also available for sale on our site.

broadview press
www.broadviewpress.com

The interior of this book is printed on 100% recycled paper.